# *Let Us Die Like Men*
## THE BATTLE OF FRANKLIN
### NOVEMBER 30, 1864

by William Lee White

EMERGING CIVIL WAR SERIES

AMERICAN
BATTLEFIELD
TRUST ★ ★ ★

PRESERVE. EDUCATE. INSPIRE.

*Chris Mackowski, series editor*
*Chris Kolakowski, chief historian*

## The Emerging Civil War Series

offers compelling, easy-to-read overviews of some of the Civil War's most important battles and stories.

*Recipient of the Army Historical Foundation's Lieutenant General Richard G. Trefry Award for contributions to the literature on the history of the U.S. Army*

### Also part of the Emerging Civil War Series:

*The Aftermath of Battle: The Burial of the Civil War Dead*
        by Meg Groeling

*All Hell Can't Stop Them: The Battles for Chattanooga: Missionary Ridge and Ringgold, Nov. 24-27, 1863*
        by David A. Powell

*All the Fighting They Want: The Atlanta Campaign, from Peachtree Creek to the Surrender of the City, July 18-September 2, 1864*
        by Stephen Davis

*Battle Above the Clouds: The Lifting the Siege of Chattanooga and the Battle of Lookout Mountain, October 16 - November 24, 1863*
        by David A. Powell

*Bushwhacking on a Grand Scale: The Battle of Chickamauga, Sept. 18-20, 1863*
        by William Lee White

*A Long and Bloody Task: The Atlanta Campaign, from Dalton to Kennesaw to the Chattahooche, May 5-July 18, 1864*
        by Stephen Davis

### For a complete list of titles in the Emerging Civil War Series, visit www.emergingcivilwar.com.

### Also by William Lee White:

*Great Things Are Expected of Us: The Letters of Colonel C. Irvine Walker, 10th South Carolina Infantry CSA.* William Lee White and Charles Denny Runion, editors. (University of Tennessee Press, 2007)

# Let Us Die Like Men

## THE BATTLE OF FRANKLIN
### NOVEMBER 30, 1864

by William Lee White

EMERGING CIVIL WAR SERIES

AMERICAN
BATTLEFIELD
TRUST ★ ★ ★

PRESERVE. EDUCATE. INSPIRE.

SB
Savas Beatie
California

Third edition, first printing

ISBN-13 (paperback): 978-1-61121-296-9
ISBN-13 (ebook): 978-1-61121-297-6

Library of Congress Cataloging-in-Publication Data

Names: White, William Lee, author.
Title: Let us die like men : the Battle of Franklin, November 30, 1864 / by William Lee White.
Description: First edition. | El Dorado Hills, California : Savas Beatie, 2018. | Series: Emerging Civil War series
Identifiers: LCCN 2017046514| ISBN 9781611212969 (pbk : alk. paper) ISBN 9781611212976 (ebk)
Subjects: LCSH: Franklin, Battle of, Franklin, Tenn., 1864.
Classification: LCC E477.52 .W48 2017 | DDC 973.7/37--dc23
LC record available at https://lccn.loc.gov/2017046514


Printed and bound in the United Kingdom


SB
Savas Beatie LLC
989 Governor Drive, Suite 102
El Dorado Hills, California 95762
916-941-6896
sales@savasbeatie.com
www.savasbeatie.com

AMERICAN
BATTLEFIELD
TRUST ★ ★ ★
PRESERVE. EDUCATE. INSPIRE.

Savas Beatie titles are available at special discounts for bulk purchases in the United States by corporations, institutions, and other organizations. For more details, e-mail us at sales@savasbeatie.com or visit our website at www.savasbeatie.com for additional information.

Dedication:

To the two strongest women I know, Nikki and Caroline.

# Foreword to the Special Preservation Edition

In November 1864, John Bell Hood's Confederate Army of Tennessee launched an assault against the combined Union Army of the Ohio and Army of the Cumberland in the Battle of Franklin. Desperate to cripple Federal forces, Hood's attack proved a disastrous Confederate defeat, resulting in some of the most brutal combat imaginable.

Regarded long after as "Bloody Franklin," and a last gasp of the Confederacy, the battle's significance cannot be overstated as one of the most savage and consequential of the war.

By the early 2000s, the battlefield was essentially destroyed, lost almost entirely to development—residential homes, strip malls, and pizza parlors marred the landscape where soldiers fought, bled, and died.

But in the last twenty years, the American Battlefield Trust has worked with state and local preservation groups to reclaim and preserve the battlefield. Some have called this national battlefield preservation effort a "miracle." Led by Franklin's Charge, Inc., the Battle for Franklin Trust, the State of Tennessee, the City of Franklin, the Tennessee Civil War National Heritage Area, and a variety of other local preservation groups, hallowed ground that was once lost is today the epitome of an American history preservation success story.

The Trust is honored to partner with Savas Beatie and its Emerging Civil War Series on this exceptional study of the Battle of Franklin. I hope you find it as insightful as I have and will join me in appreciating just how important our work—to preserve the land where America's most compelling stories unfolded—truly is.

With deepest gratitude,

David Duncan
President

# Table of Contents

*List of Maps*

*Maps by Hal Jespersen*

# *Acknowledgments*

Approaching the railroad, Loring's men suffered heavily from artillery fire in their front and from Fort Granger. (wlw)

Although most of my focus has, for many years, been the battle of Chickamauga, it was not the only battle that fueled my interest in the Civil War. One engagement that struck a cord with me was the battle of Franklin. The high drama of that engagement struck me on my first visit there with my Aunt Elaine and Uncle James at an early age. That visit remains with me still, and I owe Elaine and James a special thank you, along with my mom and dad.

I also need to thank those who helped me learn more about the battlefield over the years, either through their research or through battlefield tramping. Eric Jacobson, Thomas Cartwright, and David Fraley are at the top of that list, but also Tim Burgesss and Ronny Mangrum. Also thanks to Steven Cone for his research into Johnson's night attack, Eugene D. Schmiel for his work on Jacob Cox, Stephen "Sam" Hood for getting me to reconsider General Hood, Bob Jenkins for looking at what happened on the Eastern Flank, Don Troiani for his paintings, and Wiley Sword for his beautiful narrative that—though I don't always agree with it—helped fire my passion for this story. Also, Willie Ray Johnson, Dennis Kelly, Patrick Craddock, Kristen McClelland, Keith Bohannon, Mauriel Joslyn, Rebecca Jordan, Robert Parker, Dr. Patrick Lewis, Chris Young, Evan Jones, Chad Gray and many others.

At Savas Beatie, a huge thank you to Theodore P. Savas for once again giving me the opportunity to write this story. Thank you to his staff, as well, for all their support in making this book a reality.

At Emerging Civil War, thank you to all my fellow authors and especially Chris Mackowski for helping me with editing, words of encouragement, and suggestions.

(Chris offers an additional thanks to Greg Wade of the Franklin Civil War Round Table for showing him around the battlefield on a photo expedition.)

**Winstead Hill Park outside Franklin** (cm)

Finally, thank you once again to Nikki Ellis and Lynith for encouragement and inspiration at overcoming the odds. Along those lines I would be remiss without also acknowledging my dear friend, Caroline Eiko Lewis—you have no idea how much I respect you. To my favorite band, The Birthday Massacre (Sara, you inspire me) for, as always, being the soundtrack to my writing. Also, a thank you to Brianna Powell, Joe Blunt, Jeff Hodnett, Kris Tinney, Chuck Dunn, Rob Hodge, Heath Matthews, Joe Walker, Dave Powell, my NPS Family, John Pagano, Fred Rickard, Doug Cubbison, and all those who made the Mean Jean Machine a reality back in 1995. Thanks to Dr. Daryl Black, Myers Brown, Jim Ogden, Shane Sealy, Mike Bub, Robert Carter, Richard Manion, Mark Hendry, Lindsey Brown, John Schwarz, Marshall Burnett, Kim Calamos, Ben Wolk, Jim Lewis, and many more who I fail to list here.

*For the Emerging Civil War Series*

Theodore P. Savas, *publisher*
Chris Mackowski, *series editor*
Chris Kolakowski, *chief historian*
Sarah Keeney, *editorial consultant*
Kristopher D. White, *emeritus editor*

Maps by Hal Jespersen
Design and layout by Tara Hatmaker

3D II

# HOOD AND SCHOFIELD

NOV. 30, 1864

Schofield, slipping his army past Hood's at Spring Hill, entrenched in the southern edge of Franklin 2 mi. N. Here Hood attacked him frontally about 4 p.m., sustaining heavy losses. Schofield withdrew to Nashville. Hood followed. Hood's command post during the battle was on the slope 50 yds. west.

TENNESSEE HISTORICAL COMMISSION

"[I]f we are to die, let us die like men."
—Maj. Gen. Patrick Cleburne, C.S.A.

GEORGIA 1776

## CONFEDERATE ARMY OF TENNESSEE

The Army of Tennessee of abandoned Atlanta
Sept. 2, 1864, moved to LoveJoy, then to
Palmetto, Sept. 19. Most of the Army entrenched
3 miles N. Gen. John B. Hood had headquarters
here from Sept. 19 to 29, 1864. Pres. Jefferson
Davis visited here Sept. 25th and on the
26th made a speech to the troops 3 miles N.
where he was serenaded by the 20th Louisiana
Band. That same night Gen. Howell Cobb and
Gov. Isham Harris of Tenn. spoke. On the 27th
Pres. Davis left for Montgomery. Gen. Hardee
was relieved of his command here. Sept. 28,
and on the 29th Gen. Hood moved from here to
start the disastrous Tennessee Campaign.

# Some Fighting and Some Hard Marching

## CHAPTER ONE
### *September 1864*

On September 1, 1864, Gen. William Tecumseh Sherman's Union armies sealed the fate of Atlanta when they severed the last rail line into the city.

That evening, Confederate Lt. Gen. William J. Hardee—whose command was overwhelmed with heavy losses at Jonesboro—notified his commander in Atlanta, Gen. John Bell Hood, that the last supply line into the city was lost.

Hood was, in many ways, the living personification of the Confederacy at this point. Having lost a leg at Chickamauga and having never fully regained the use of a wounded arm after Gettysburg, Hood still had a spark to fight on. With his back against the gates of Atlanta, he took command of the Army of Tennessee after Confederate President Jefferson Davis relieved the previous commander, Gen. Joseph E. Johnston, from command. Hood then launched a series of actions to try to save the city, actions that—though sound and even brilliant in concept—failed to give him the results he desired—and needed—to save it. Although he was a student in the offensive-minded "Lee and Jackson School," he was unable to get the army he commanded to work in the same fashion. Having no alternative after the fall of Jonesboro, Hood ordered his troops to abandon the city and destroy all supplies that could not be removed.

As Hood's men marched south to join Hardee,

**At the end of the Atlanta Campaign, John Bell Hood placed his army at the end of one of their last supply lines at Palmetto, Georgia. There, he began to formulate the plan that would lead to his Tennessee campaign. (wlw)**

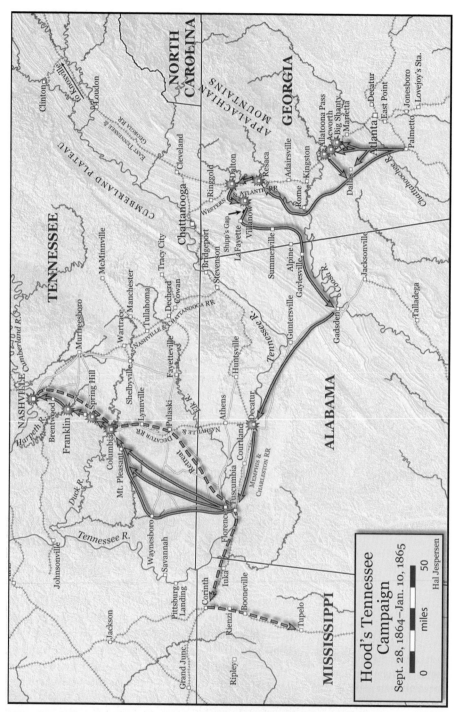

HOOD'S TENNESSEE CAMPAIGN—After failing to dislodge Sherman's armies by harassing their supply line, John Bell Hood swung his Army of Tennessee westward through Alabama and made a run at Sherman's supply base at Nashville. Along the way, he attacked whatever Federal forces he could find, which led to attrition in his own army that he could ill afford.

they were serenaded by explosions of their burning ordinance, which cast an eerie glow in the sky behind them that could be seen for miles.

Hardee, meanwhile, retreated with his corps from Jonesboro six miles south to the vicinity of Lovejoy Station, where they halted about a mile north of the town and were ordered to entrench along a low ridge known as Cedar Bluffs. The ridge was bordered on its east and west sides by streams and marshy ground, making it an ideal defensive position.

Upon learning of Hardee's retreat, Sherman ordered Maj. Gen. George Henry Thomas to pursue. Soon after 10 a.m. on September 2, the Federal vanguard arrived in front of Hardee's Confederates. The Union forces began to deploy and scout the Confederate line. Observing the position, Sherman noted that the Confederate works were strong—and he could see that they were still working on them. Knowing the fortifications were getting stronger by the minute, and thinking the Confederates were demoralized, he considered offering immediate battle, but then reconsidered. Atlanta was his after a grueling campaign, and there was no need to add to the casualties. The following day, Sherman telegraphed Washington: "Atlanta is ours and fairly won."

John Bell Hood didn't desire the command of the Army of Tennessee. His promotion to head of the army put him in a hopeless situation: backed up against the outskirts of Atlanta, he was expected to save the city. (loc)

\*    \*    \*

The end of the campaign offered a brief moment of respite for Hood and his ragged Army of Tennessee, which was a shadow of its former

After several bloody battles, a month-long siege, and the Confederate evacuation, little remained of the city of Atlanta. (loc)

Confederate Lt. Gen. William J. Hardee was known as "Old Reliable." However, his conduct under General Hood's leadership proved problematic because he resented the younger man's promotion over him at the gates of Atlanta. (loc)

self. The Atlanta campaign had nearly bled it dry; many of its best soldiers and officers lay buried in red Georgia clay from Jonesboro to Dalton.

The campaign had also seen dramatic changes in the face of the war. The men had started the campaign as novices in the entrenching game, quickly transforming into experts at digging, living in the trenches, and judging the strength of works.

Hood marched the army to the head of a new supply line on the West Point and Atlanta Railroad at the little town of Palmetto, Georgia, located on the railroad about 25 miles southwest of Atlanta. He then went to work on a number of tasks trying to restore what he could of the army by rebuilding his officer corps, consolidating depleted regiments, and repairing its morale. He also found himself facing two difficult situations: deciding what to do next, and exorcising a ghost that had haunted his army almost since the day it first took to the field—the dysfunctional nature of the high command. The relationship between Hood and the last of the army's longtime corps commanders, General Hardee, had reached the breaking point during the struggle for Atlanta. Hardee's performance had failed to live up to his nickname, "Old Reliable," and Hood now demanded Hardee's removal, blaming him for the loss of the city. Hardee, meanwhile, let his feelings about Hood be known to anyone who would listen—including Davis. "I told him that things had reached a point when it was necessary for him to relieve either Hood or myself," Hardee said of his conversation with the Confederate president, "that I did not ask him to relieve Hood, but insisted on his relieving me."

All of this, especially the return of the infighting among the army's leadership, convinced President Jefferson Davis that he must go to Georgia to investigate and attempt a resolution. This would be the third time he'd had to go to his western army for essentially the same problem.

Davis arrived in Palmetto on September

Union Maj. Gen. William T. Sherman, the victor of struggle for Atlanta, was initially baffled at his opponent's move into his rear. (loc)

**Detachments of Union troops garrisoned blockhouses similar to this one up and down the length of the Western and Atlantic Railroad.** (loc)

25th. Over the next few days, he inspected the troops, interviewed the army's generals about the controversy, and conferred with Hood about what the army should do next.

Among his major decisions, Davis created a new department, the Military Division of the West, to be commanded by Gen. P. G. T. Beauregard, and then placed the Army of Tennessee in the division, essentially giving Hood a supervisor. The Confederate president also decided to keep Hood in command, which meant that Hardee had to go because he refused to continue serving under Hood. Davis transferred Hardee, and Maj. Gen. Benjamin Franklin Cheatham took command of the corps.

In matters of strategy, Cheatham always supported an offense, so he heartily approved of the plan Hood formulated. Hood proposed to seize the initiative and move his army northward, strike at Sherman's supply lines and communications, and force him to abandon Atlanta, then confront him somewhere in the mountainous terrain of northwest Georgia. But Sherman was expecting such a move. Davis had broadcast the Confederate intentions in a number of speeches he made while on his trip. Those intentions found their way into the

**Confederate President Jefferson Davis found his way to visit the Army of Tennessee at Palmetto to investigate the problems that seemed to haunt the Confederacy's western army.** (loc)

General Alexander P. Stewart moved his corps to strike at the railroads near Kennesaw Mountain. (bsaot)

newspapers and then into Sherman's hands. The only question was when and where.

Sherman had been hoping to go on the offensive first, wishing to move his army toward the coast, but he took some precautions. He sent Maj. Gen. George Thomas to Chattanooga with Maj. Gen. David Stanley's IV Corps; he ordered Brig. Gen. John M. Corse to take his division of the XVI Corps to Rome, Georgia, to bolster the garrison there; and he sent word to all the garrisons, both large and small, along the railroad to be on the lookout for the Confederates.

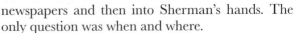

*    *    *

The Army of Tennessee crossed over the Chattahoochee on September 29, and then turned to the north and northeast, toward the Western and Atlantic Railroad. Lieutenant General Stephen D. Lee and Maj. Gen. Benjamin Franklin Cheatham moved their corps toward the old battlefields of the "Hell Hole," where they had fought three battles near the town of Dallas, Georgia, the previous May. The return brought a shroud of melancholy over the troops. Seeing the devastation, one soldier jotted in his diary, "Country here totally destroyed. No signs of civilization." Another remembered the graves of their fallen, which "after the elapse of three months or more we could sometimes see a hand and probably a part of an arm or a foot and maybe a part of a leg, again we would see one or both knees exposed . . . ."

To improve the army's mood, Hood asked some of his officers to speak to the men about the campaign. One Texan remembered hearing "that we were going to flank Sherman out of Atlanta, and in maneuvering we might be short of rations occasionally, but that he (Genl Hood) would do his best on that point. That he expected to have some fighting and some hard marching, and wanted an expression of the men upon it. Of course every man said go."

Major General Patrick Cleburne spoke to a large crowd of soldiers. One Floridian recalled the speech:

General Alexander Reynolds led his Arkansas brigade against the Union blockhouse at Moon Station, Georgia. (nps)

*He urged every man to do his whole duty, to stand firm by the righteous cause they had espoused. He pictured to us Ireland in its downfallen and trampled condition and told us if we failed our condition would be much worse than that of Ireland's, as long as that spirit of hate and revenge lived in the North. In closing the address that night he turned his face toward the skies and with the fervency of his soul he exclaimed, 'If this cause that is so dear to my heart is doomed to fail, I pray heaven may let me fall with it, while my face is toward the enemy and my arm battling for that which I know to be right.*

Small garrisons protected Sherman's line, the Western and Atlantic Railroad. Hood's first strike was at the garrison at Big Shanty. (wlw)

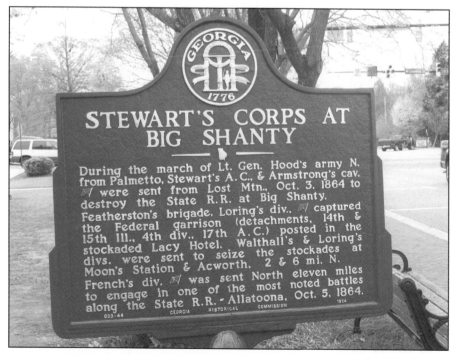

State historical markers now offer the only reminders of the small but intense fights that were a hallmark of Hood's move through North Georgia. (wlw)

**The Army of Tennessee retraced its route to Atlanta, passing under the shadow of their former positions on the heights of Kennesaw Mountain.** (wlw)

This would be a harbinger of things to come for Cleburne and many of the soldiers who heard him speak.

Lieutenant General Alexander P. Stewart's corps was ordered along with Brig. Gen. William Hicks "Red" Jackson's cavalry division—the only cavalry Hood still retained after Maj. Gen. Joseph Wheeler took the bulk of the cavalry corps into Sherman's rear in August—to move on the towns of Big Shanty and Acworth and strike the railroad there, after capturing the towns' garrisons. The capture of each village proved easy, as the odds were overwhelmingly against the Union garrisons—what James Binford termed, "Our glorious bloodless victory."

Wheeler's cavalry had not returned from this campaign. Instead Wheeler had led his men into east Tennessee and then middle Tennessee, a foray causing minimal damage yet depriving Hood of his "eyes and ears" during a critical stage of the struggle for Atlanta. As a new campaign started, Hood remained largely blind and deaf.

"To Destroy is a soldier's joy," said Capt. Joseph Boyce of the 1st Missouri. If Boyce was right, joy must have prevailed along the lines as Stewart's men proceeded to destroy the Western and Atlantic

Railroad. Boyce went on to describe it: "Huge fires of ties were built," and in the words of Ordinance Sgt. William Smith: "The country was one blaze of light for miles along the burning rail road." Around Big Shanty, Acworth, and Moon Station, the railroad was effectively torn up. "The ties burned and rails bent for a distance of ten or twelve miles," reported Stewart. The Confederates captured more than 600 prisoners, adding the garrisons' stores of ammunition and rations to their haul.

Things were off to a good start for Hood, so he sent orders to Stewart for a more ambitious plan.

# A Needless Effusion of Blood
## The Fight at Allatoona Pass

## CHAPTER TWO
### Early October 1864

Now with several successes under his belt, Hood saw a larger target looming: the Allatoona Pass.

The man-made pass had been cut through the mountain in the 1840s and was the deepest cut on the Western and Atlantic Railroad between Chattanooga and Atlanta. The pass had already seen much during the war. The Great Locomotive Chase sped through in 1862, and earlier in 1864, Joe Johnston constructed such a formidable defensive position there that Sherman decided to flank it instead, leading to the fighting near New Hope Church, which became known as the "Hell Hole." With Johnston's withdrawal, Union forces managing Sherman's supply route made the little village a major supply depot, constructing warehouses and fortifications to guard them and the critical pass.

The pass was now a target for Hood. Destroying it would effectively break Sherman's supply line. General Stewart received the orders for one more foray.

Stewart was to send a division to destroy the gap and the equally important railroad bridge over the Etowah River, a few miles to the north. The mission went to Maj. Gen. Samuel Gibbs French and his small division of 3,276 Missourians, Mississippians, Texans, and North Carolinians, plus a battalion of artillery under the command of Maj. John Myrick. French received his orders at noon on October 4, but due to delays, he wasn't able to begin his march until around 3:00 p.m. Securing a local guide and ominously hearing "the enemy had fortifications

Allatoona Pass was an important forward supply depot for Sherman's army as well as the critical choke point on the Western and Atlantic railroad. If destroyed, it could be a huge setback for Sherman. (loc)

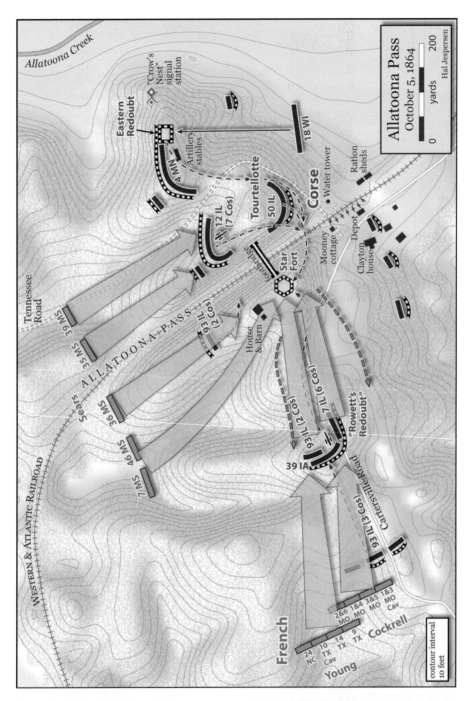

**Allatoona Pass**
October 5, 1864

Hal Jespersen

0    yards    200

contour interval
10 feet

**ALLATOONA PASS**—The Battle of Allatoona was a savage but small engagement that set the tone for what happened in Tennessee a few weeks later. Confederates made a desperate charge against an entrenched foe, some of whom were armed with repeating rifles, creating irreplaceable losses in the already-diminished Confederate ranks.

at Allatoona, well garrisoned," French moved out, arriving in the village of Ackworth as the October sun set. Once again there was a delay, caused this time as his men waited until 11:00 p.m. to receive their rations.

Obtaining a guide—a cavalryman who was from the area—French moved his division northeast toward the Allatoona Hills and away from the rest of his parent corps. The division marched nearly uninterrupted through the night until, near Allatoona Creek, he came across a Union blockhouse that guarded the railroad. Not wishing to lose any more time, French detached the 4th Mississippi and one cannon to deal with the blockhouse and its garrison. Continuing on with the rest of his men, French arrived on the south side of Allatoona Pass at 3 a.m. There, for the first time, they stood before their target looming in the darkness. Only flickering lights from the garrison, visible in the pitch black of the night, told of the Union soldiers' presence.

Preparations for the attack now began. French sent word to his artillery under the command of Maj. Myrick to deploy his batteries on the high ground there: a low hill with an open northern slope about 1,200 yards from the pass, known as Moore's Hill. Myrick's 10 guns unlimbered in the cleared space, and French ordered the 32nd Texas and the 39th North Carolina from Young's brigade to deploy in their support.

French now weighed his options. A frontal attack against the twin Union forts would be a disaster, so he decided to strike the western flank, where the terrain

Construction began on this gap in 1842. To meet state railroad grade laws, the "Deep Cut" ended up being 180 feet deep—120 feet of it through solid rock. Slave labor was used in the construction here and all along the railroad. (wlw)

offered better odds of success and where only one fort would be able to offer resistance. The challenge now was to get into position. The only road, Old Cartersville, went up to the pass before turning to the west toward its namesake, so using it was out of the question. Myrick's men would have to move overland as best they could in the darkness.

With his guide leading the way, the column moved down into a rugged series of maze-like gullies, groping along through the piney woods before the guide admitted that he was hopelessly lost. French called a halt. "I determined to rest where we were and await daylight," he later recalled.

Fate did not smile on French when the sun rose. The previous day, as French had struggled with his frustrating delays, Union Brig. Gen. John M. Corse had been on his way to Allatoona. On October 4, Corse had received word to take part of his command back down the railroad to reinforce the Union garrison at Allatoona. Just a short time prior, Corse had been ordered up from Sherman's Army to Rome, Georgia, to bolster the garrison as Hood began his new campaign. Corse loaded as many men of his division as was possible, along with 165,000 rounds of ammunition, onto 20 railroad cars and headed down the railroad, arriving at the pass just after midnight on October 5. There, he met with the garrison commander, Col. John E. Tourtellotte, who

Though this gap—"the Deep Cut"—ran countless supply trains for both the Union and the Confederacy. (wlw)

accompanied Corse as he made a hasty inspection of the defenses even as his command unloaded from the cars and deployed in the open ground south of the pass. Among them was the 7th Illinois Infantry—

recently armed with the Henry repeating rifle, a weapon that could fire 16 shots in rapid succession.

Corse, seeing what he had to work with and uncertain where the Confederate threat would come from, ordered out a screen of skirmishers, then set about deploying his troops and the garrison. He decided to have Tourtellotte command the defenses on the eastern side of the pass, and Maj. Richard Rowett took command of the western defenses. Corse soon had his men moving to the western side of the pass, moving out to occupy an earthwork that would soon become known as Rowett's Redoubt. By daybreak, Corse's men were in position and waiting for the Confederates.

**John Corse's timely arrival saved the day for the Union forces.** (loc)

French had his men up with first light and moving in the right direction. Soon, the gullies and forest began to echo with the first rounds of Myrick's guns as they began to bark their morning greeting at the Union positions. The Confederates arrived on the western edge of the ridge and began to deploy for battle.

French's plan now called for his Mississippi brigade under Brig. Gen. Claudius Sears to make its way farther to the north and come down on the pass from that direction. When that attack began, the other two brigades of the division would attack from the west, catching the defenders in a pincer.

As Sears began to move northward and the other brigades formed up to face eastward, French sent a member of his staff to demand the surrender of the post: "Sir: I have placed forces under my command in such a position that you are surrounded, and to avoid a needless effusion of blood, I call on you to surrender your forces at once and unconditionally.

**Major General Samuel G. French commanded the Confederate forces. He was not expecting the warm reception his command received at Allatoona.** (Two Wars, Samuel French)

**Union trenches seemed to cover all approaches.** (wlw)

**Confederate artillery bombarded the Union positions at Allatoona Pass.** (jb)

Five minutes will be allowed you to decide. Should you accede to this, you will be treated in the most honorable manner as prisoners of war."

The officer waited and waited, but no reply came; finally, after 15 minutes, he made his way back to the lines. As he passed the awaiting infantry, one soldier asked, "Is it surrender or fight, Major?" The curt reply was "Fight!" This episode became a point of controversy afterwards as Corse claimed to have responded with a defiant refusal, stating that he was "prepared for the 'needless effusion of blood,'" but his message was never delivered. In any event, it was all the same: there would be an effusion of blood.

During the wait, French's infantry finished up its deployments along the ridge. Brigadier General Francis Marion Cockrell's Missouri brigade formed in front, and en échelon to them was Col. William H. Young's Texas and North Carolina brigades—only around 2,000 men altogether but some of the best fighters in Confederate service. French was waiting for the sound of Sears's guns, but Sears was having a difficult time getting into position because of rough terrain. The Confederate commander decided he couldn't wait any longer and sent word for Cockrell and Young to attack. It was now a little past 10 a.m. The Missourians were called to attention and prepared to advance. They dropped their knapsacks, shifted their accouterments to better reach their cartridges and caps, and unfurled their colors. In some cases, officers offered words of encouragement to their men. Then the bugles blared, and the Missouri brigade moved forward with a purpose.

Their advance cleared away the Union skirmishers in their front and moved rapidly toward the Rowett's Redoubt. The roar of battle erupted from the rifles of the three regiments manning the redoubt and the lone smoothbore cannon posted there. Meanwhile, Confederate artillery ceased fire, and Myrick and his gunners became spectators for fear of hitting their own infantry.

The Missourians rushed forward into a storm of lead and iron, but they were forced back about 20 yards from the fortification, seeking what shelter they could among the ragged brush and stumps. From there, they began to return fire.

As the Missouri brigade made its advance, Sears's wayward Mississippians finally began their advance down a long front, rolling over the hilly ground on the north side of the pass. Colonel Young addressed his men, ordering them forward to join the Missourians. After a few minutes, Maj. Ezekiel Hampton of the 29th North Carolina jumped up and ordered his men to charge, starting a chain reaction that soon had both brigades rushing forward

**The veterans of the Missouri Brigade overran the Union positions in the first phase of the fighting.** (jb)

The Missouri monument at Allatoona, located near the entrance of the park today, is a recent addition to the battlefield. (wlw)

The Texas monument is dedicated to the men of Young's brigade, which once again proved its fighting ability at Allatoona. (wlw)

One of the recent monuments placed upon the site, the Illinois monument remembers the men of the 7th Illinois and others who fought at Allatoona Pass. (wlw)

with their rebel yells. Confederates quickly mounted the works, and vicious hand-to-hand fighting ensued with bayonets, bare fists, and even large clods of dirt. "The federals stood right up to their work, and we, for a few seconds, had what the boys call 'a hell of a time,'" noted Capt. Joseph Boyce of the 1st Missouri Infantry. "Our Texas friends . . . caught up and went over with us. As our boys swarmed over the parapet the bayonet was freely used by both sides, officers firing their pistols, and many throwing sticks and stones."

The national colors of the 39th Iowa fell into Confederate custody. Sergeant John Ragland of the 1st Missouri, remembered Captain Boyce, "with a daring leap . . . tore them from their bearers' grasp, who received a clod of hard clay . . . between the eyes at the same instant."

The appearance of Sears's Mississippians on the flank and the ferociousness of the assault forced a union retreat to the main fort. Even the 7th Illinois with their repeaters, along with the Napoleon gun that supported them, were unable to resist, despite inflicting heavy casualties. "The storm breaks upon them in all its mad fury; the Seventh is now struggling against the reckless rush of the infuriated rebels that are swarming toward their front," the regimental historian remembered. "The sixteen-shooters are doing their work; the very air seems to grow faint as it breathes their lurid flame. Colonel Rowett soon after the onset discovers a rebel regiment charging on to the right flank from the northwest, threatening to sweep it back like so much chaff. . . . It is soon discovered that it will be madness to attempt to hold the weakly constructed outer work. A retreat is ordered. . . ."

The rest of Rowett's line joined them as they rushed back and started piling into the fort and its surrounding ditch. Confederates reorganized and prepared for what they hoped would be the final push to victory.

\*     \*     \*

East of the railroad, two of Sears's regiments managed to start pushing up the slopes toward the eastern redoubt, but fire from the Union trench line halted their advance, forcing nearly 80 men to seek

shelter down in a steep ravine, where they soon found themselves trapped and unable to retreat lest they be caught in a deadly crossfire. To the south, a skirmish line from the artillery supports attempted a push to the edge of the town, but the line could not make headway, and in the end proved to be just an annoyance.

**Men of the 7th Illinois Infantry pose with their Henry repeaters.** (nps)

Back at the fort, the assaults began. Confederates found that there was still much fight in Corse's men. One of the Union defenders, a member of the Signal Corps, noted a few days later: "We all had muskets & fired away like Trojans. The rebs actually charged right up to our fort. . . . We could see the whites of their eyes, they came so close, but we beat them back. . . ."

**The Star Fort still remains an imposing sight upon the Allatoona Pass battlefield.** (wlw)

Corse himself was there and oversaw the fighting until he was wounded, passing command to Colonel Rowlett, who in turn was wounded a short time later. Then Tourtellotte took over. The Federals held on, although the inside of the fort became a scene of horror as men found themselves crammed inside to the point of almost not being able to move without stepping on a dead or wounded comrade.

**The entrance into the Star Fort as it would have appeared at the time.** (loc)

**The Clayton house, a survivor of the battle, is now private property.** (wlw)

**Bullet holes throughout the Clayton house speak of the intensity of the fire.** (wlw)

Still the Federals resisted, driving the Confederates back four times and forcing them to seek what shelter they could among the stumps and furrows of the slopes.

The fight became a long-range skirmish and sharpshooting contest, which continued to add more casualties to the growing list of fallen as it became fatal to peer over the parapet of the fort. However, the gunner of the fort's rifled cannon hit upon the idea of using percussion shells against a cluster of stumps that sat immediately beyond the area where a troublesome groups of Confederates sheltered. The shells exploded on impact and hurled shrapnel and wooden splinters into the backs of the Southerners.

The afternoon ticked on bloodily.

Finally, French received word, ultimately proven to be false, that Union forces were rapidly approaching from the south. He felt forced to break the stalemate and retreat, much to the chagrin of many of his officers and men who believed that one more assault would carry the Union defenses— doubtful, given the strength of the fort and the losses Confederates had already experienced.

French's men fell back and began their withdrawal. The fight had indeed been a needless effusion of blood. French lost almost 800 men killed and wounded, though Corse wasn't far behind with slightly more than 700 casualties. The battle had been intense and desperate, especially considering the numbers involved. As a testament to that: of the 165,000 rounds Corse brought to the fight, only 250 were left.

French did have consolation, though, as he traced his way back toward Acworth. He brought the might of his division upon the stubborn block house at Allatoona Creek, which had managed to hold on all day against the 4th Mississippi and the lone cannon left there earlier. The blockhouse fell, and its small garrison was soon on its way to captivity.

French continued back to join Stewart's Corps. Corse and his command had managed to win a tough-fought victory—one that would become the stuff of legend and even lead to a popular hymn based on a message wigwagged to the garrison's signal station from the heights of Kennesaw Mountain. The message, from General Sherman, said, "Hold On, I am coming."

Though a bloody setback, Hood was not stopping.

**Looking over the walls of the Star Fort in the direction of the Confederate attacks.** (wlw)

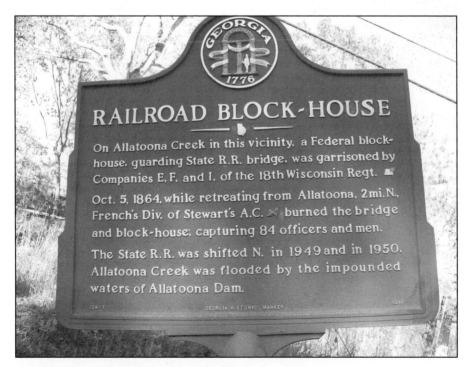

**A state historical marker tells the story of the fight for the blockhouse.** (wlw)

# Immediate and Unconditional Surrender

## The Return to Resaca and Dalton

### CHAPTER THREE
*Mid October 1864*

French's defeat at Allatoona did not deter Hood. Once his army was reunited near the former New Hope Church battlefield, Hood continued pushing his army northward. When the army reached Cave Springs, General Beauregard overtook them and, on October 9, had his first face-to-face meeting with Hood about his campaign.

As a result, Beauregard stepped into a logistical support role by heading to Gadsden, Alabama, to set up a supply base there for the army while Hood took steps to lighten his army. He ordered the bulk of the army's wagon train and most of the artillery to move westward to Jacksonville, Alabama, near Gadsden.

Bolstered by the return of Wheeler and his cavalry, Hood moved to threaten Rome, although he did not attack the town itself because it was too heavily defended. Only a badly managed cavalry battle ensued, which became known as the "Rome Races," while the Confederate cavalry tried to screen the army's movement from the Union garrison there.

The Army of Tennessee swung around to the west, crossing the Coosa River on a pontoon bridge a few miles west of Rome on October 10. Then it moved eastward back toward Resaca, where another opportunity to damage Sherman's supply lines lay with the railroad bridge over the Oostanaula River.

The village of Resaca and the bridge were

The Army of Tennesse had been to Resaca the previous spring, where they slugged it out with Federal forces May 13-15, 1864. Their return engagement on October 12 proved much smaller. (cm)

Col. Clark R. Wever of the 17th Iowa commanded the Union garrison at Resaca, overseeing the town and the important railroad bridge located there. (ia)

Union forces built a redoubt on the former Confederate Fort Wayne, guarding the Railroad bridge at Resaca. The walls are still visible today. (wlw)

protected by a large fortified complex consisting of Forts Phillips, Braden, and Lane—one being the remains of an old Confederate fort known as Fort Wayne, although that structure was now gone, having been cannibalized into another much larger and more complex series of fortifications around the town. The garrison, under the command of Col. Clark R. Wever, consisted of only two small regiments of infantry, totaling 710 men. Wever had four Napoleons captured from the Cherokee Light Artillery the previous spring in the first Battle of Resaca that had been pressed into service by detachments of infantrymen.

Arriving on October 12, Hood accompanied his old corps, now under Lt. Gen. Stephen D. Lee, to invest the town and fort. "The first symptom . . . of the enemy's advance on the place was the appearance of a few cavalrymen, skirmishing without pickets," recalled the chaplain of the 80th Ohio. "There were several shots exchanged, but nothing to signify the strength of the enemy, until about 2 o'clock, when the rebels . . . commenced planting batteries in conspicuous positions, and deploying a line of skirmishers in front of our defenses. For an hour shots were exchanged freely from both sides, whenever opportunity offered. Scouts were sent out, and reinforcements soon arrived. The rebel sharpshooters fired from trees with murderous aim . . . ."

Lee brought forward nearly 7,000 men. Things looked bleak for Wever, who took the step of having the garrison's band and other non-combatants armed and brought into the defenses—but he still mustered only a little more than 600.

At 4 p.m., Hood sent a dire demand of surrender to the post's commander: "Sir—I demand the immediate & unconditional surrender of the post & garrison under your command. If these terms

Looking west from within the Union lines at Resaca, where Confederates made their first appearance before the town. (wlw)

are acceded to, all white officers and soldiers will be paroled in a few days. If the place is carried by assault, no prisoners will be taken."

Col. Wever's reply left no doubt: "Your communication of this date is just received, its contents have been noted, and after expressing my indignation and surprise at your barbarous threat, allow me to say that I am able to hold this post, and will hold it against your forces, and will not surrender it, no never."

These Confederate trenches were built in May 1864 and were once again occupied during the standoff at Resaca in October. (wlw)

"As soon as that reply was sent out," one of Wever's officers recorded, "firing commenced. . . ." One observer noted, "He formed line of battle, extending from the river on the left entirely around the place to the river on the right." Wever faced a grim prospect as the autumn sun made its way lower in the western sky, but then the cavalry arrived—literally. Colonel Louis T. Watkins's brigade of 500 Kentucky cavalrymen dismounted and crossed over the railroad bridge. They had moved up from Calhoun when Watkins learned of Hood's presence at Resaca. The cavalrymen immediately went into action on Wever's right, driving back the encircling Confederates in that area. Sharpshooting and cannon fire echoed over the surrounding hills as twilight slowly covered the battlefield in darkness.

During the night, a handful of Federal reinforcements—some 350 more men—arrived from the south along with Gen. Green Raum. Federals also used the cover of dark to develop a clever ruse. Looking everywhere they could, they rounded up every flag in the area and had them posted at points along the works. "The next morning there was a heavy fog, and when it raised there were revealed to the astonished gaze of the rebels twenty seven flags floating upon our works," one Federal remembered. "Everything in the shape of a flag that could be raised had been put out, a brass band was playing national airs, and the solders were shouting defiance to the rebels."

Louis Watkins, born in Florida, commanded a brigade of Kentucky cavalry that spent a large amount of time in the North Georgia mountains fighting guerillas in the summer of 1864. Watkins brought timely reinforcements to the beleaguered garrison at Resaca. (na)

The sudden appearance of so many flags caused the Confederates to balk. Then word came that Sherman was approaching again, as had happened at Allatoona—except this time it proved to be true. Hood decided Resaca wasn't worth it and ordered Lee to move his corps westward toward Snake Creek Gap and to take up a defensive position there with

Stewart's efforts targeted the railroad between Tilton and Resaca. (wlw)

part of his forces and move on to the community of Villanow with the rest. Hood himself departed and headed north to join Cheatham's Corps at Dalton

\*    \*    \*

As Lee faced Resaca, Stewart's Corps moved to strike the railroad above Resaca. After a short but determined fight, they captured a railroad workers' camp a short distance from the village and then forced the surrender of the Union blockhouse at Tilton when they struck at the railroad yet again. "We saw the fires along the railroad north of us, and knew that the work of destruction was being pushed without pause," General Raum recalled.

Cheatham's Corps marched on toward Dalton, striking at the railroad south of town before moving on to confront the Union garrison of the town. The situation at Dalton was a smoldering powder keg. The majority of the garrison consisted of men of the 44th United States Colored Troops, a regiment of runaway formerly enslaved men from North Georgia and Tennessee formed in Chattanooga earlier that year. The garrison occupied a fort that held four bronze cannon, built upon a ridge running along the eastern side of town. Confederates soon surrounded them. Again Hood sent in the same demand for surrender or risk no quarter.

Confederate infantry assaulted Union-defended blockhouse. This scene was repeated several times—such as at Tilton and Buzzard Roost—as Hood made his way through North Georgia. (jb)

But trouble was brewing within Hood's ranks. Word spread through the Confederates that a large portion of the garrison was made up of the 44th USCT. An Arkansas soldier later remembered that as some of the troops deployed, they began to pass this word down the line: "Kill every damn one of them."

Colonel Lewis Johnson of the 44th at first resisted Hood's demands, but as skirmishing began and artillery battalions deployed west and south of the fort, Johnson agreed to a meeting with the Confederate commander. Hood "pointed out S. D. Lee's

corps, Frank Cheatham's corps, and insinuated that still another corps lay within call; fifty pieces of cannon eyed . . . from different points of the compass. Johnson begged that all might be made prisoners of war." Hood replied that "he could not restrain his men, and would not if he could." Johnson seeing that he had very little choice—"we were surrounded"—surrendered the fort and his command, the largest surrender of USCT troops during the war.

Small blockhouses were strategically placed at passes and bridges down the Western and Atlantic Railroad to protect it from Confederate cavalry raiders and guerillas. (wlw)

A tense situation followed as recorded by a white officer in the 44th. "As soon as the terms of surrender were made known my men flocked around me and asked if I thought their lives would be spared or if they would be murdered as some knew at Fort Pillow . . ." recalled Lt. Morris Hall. "I could not answer them positively, but quieted their fears as much as possible."

Morris and his fellow officers were soon separated from their men as Confederates began to divide up the formerly enslaved men, stripping them "of their overcoats and hats," and then "under guard and lash" set them to work tearing up the railroad track. William Bevins of the 1st Arkansas later wrote, "The prisoners were put to work at tearing up the railroad track. One of the negroes protested against the work as he was a sergeant. When he had paid the penalty for disobeying orders the rest tore up the road readily and rapidly."

Ugly incidents were unavoidable. Patrick Cleburne wrote in his diary, "Our men were very bitter on the negroes and the officers hollering to the latter to kiss their brothers. A great many of the men think that negroes ought not to be taken prisoner and in case of a fight I think they will catch it." Reflecting this, an Alabamian noted, "the boys were anxious to massacre these fellows, and the officers had a hard time to keep the men from falling on them."

Indeed, Spencer Tally, a Confederate officer described some of what happened:

The community of Tilton witnessed several events during the war, notably the Great Locomotive Chase and the October 1864 engagement. This sign tells both stories. (wlw)

*We took the white men as prisoners, but the negroes were taken as livestock. . . . The separation of these white officers from their negro commands was as interesting as well as a sickening scene to our southern boys. The white officers in bidding farewell*

**Stewart formed his command before the blockhouse at Tilton in these fields.** (wlw)

**A recent wayside marker tells the story of the events that occurred in Dalton in October of 1864.** (wlw)

with their colored men showed in no uncertain way their love and devotion to the colored race. Their hearty handshakes and expressions of sorrow over their separation will never be forgotten.

*The Macon Daily Telegraph* crowed over the former slaves: "They will not be treated as prisoners of war, but if any of them should live long they will be reduced to their normal condition."

\* \* \*

Once the destruction of the railroad was completed, Hood ordered his forces to move westward, with a portion passing over Rocky Face Ridge at Dug Gap and the other through Mill Creek Gap, where Bate's division had captured and destroyed a Union blockhouse.

But with Sherman now in close proximity, the campaign took on a new turn. Soon, the Union pursuit began to clash with the rear elements of Hood's army. One fight occurred at Snake Creek Gap as Lee's Corps moved westward.

The Army of Tennessee came back together briefly at the little village of Villanow, where the white USCT officers were released but the black enlisted men were corralled into a corner of the crossroads while notice was sent out for locals to

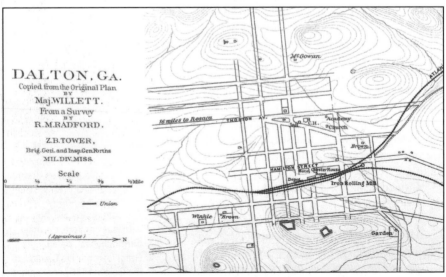

**This map from the Official Records displays the Union fortifications constructed around Dalton after it fell into Union hands the previous spring.** (loc)

come claim their "property." Those not claimed that day continued on with the army, in essence becoming enslaved by the Confederate army unless later claimed by someone as their "property." Some ultimately ended up being forced to construct fortifications at Mobile or repairing decrepit railroads in north Mississippi.

Looking westward to Ship's Gap where a small but intense rear-guard fight occurred as Sherman's vanguard finally caught up with Hood after Sherman and Hood played a cat and mouse game among the ridges of northwest Georgia. (wlw)

With Sherman closing in, Hood ordered his forces to split up again in an attempt to confuse Sherman as to which was the main column. "We have fared scantily at times for rations and the marching has been rapid and long indeed," noted Archie Livingston of the 3rd Florida in Bate's division. "The spirit of the troops was never better. No straggling at all. . . .We march from day light to dark, making sometimes 15 to 20 miles per day."

However, a vise was now tightening on the Confederates as Union forces moved south from Chattanooga and north from Rome. Hood jockeyed to find a place to do battle, but the numbers were quickly mounting against him as the rear guards of his forces clashed with the Union forces at Shipp's Gap and Treadway's Gap. "A few shots were fired from our division battery to open up the fight when the troops advanced as rapidly as the nature of the ground would permit," an officer in the 76th Ohio recalled of the fight at Shipp's Gap. "The Rebels were kept so busy . . . in front that they were not aware of the presence of our boys on their flanks until they closed in so rapidly that few could escape." Although a small fight, the rear guard action cost the defenders: Col. Ellison Capers of the

Col. Lewis Johnson, a Prussian immigrant, served in the 10th Indiana Infantry, where he rose from private to captain before taking a commission with the newly formed 44th United States Colored Troops at Chattanooga in the spring of 1864. (chch)

**Pvt. Hubbard Pryor, pictured here in before-and-after photographs for his enlistment in the 44th USCT, was captured with most of his regiment at Dalton and returned to enslavement by the Confederate army.** (loc)

24th South Carolina reported losing 4 officers and 40 men.

Hood continued on to LaFayette, bringing back more memories to some of his men: "[P]assing through a gap and recognizing some places where we had been before . . ." a member of the 33rd Alabama recalled as they passed over Taylor's Ridge; "[N]ear LaFayette, camped at the same place where we had bivouacked one night in September, 1863, just before the battle of Chickamauga." General Cleburne also remembered and compared the appearance of LaFayette upon his second arrival there on October 15:

**The Union garrison at Dalton overlooked the town on its east side. In August, the garrison withstood a Confederate cavalry raid. In October, they would not be so fortunate.** (wlw)

*This once pretty village is a wreck now. The Court House, roughly pierced with port holes and spattered all over with bullet marks, is doorless and windowless. All the adjacent houses torn to shreds-irregular conglomerations of plank shelters- half finished, half ruined intrenchments-deserted houses-all the fencing and paling gone. I put up at Church. It had evidently been used and misused by the enemy. A platform for theatricals was at one end. Its walls were defaced all over with yankee names. Horse dung was on its floor. But latterly it must have been deserted by the yanks, for dead butterflies and half devoured birds lay about on the floor and spiders had built their webs across the entrance. I took my headquarters at an empty, but picturesque cottage half a mile out on the Chattanooga road. The little gate was open, but creeping rose bushes almost barred entrance to the open rooms. Doves were roosting (for it was after sunset,) in the apple trees that darkened the windows, The vines on the supports could be seen above the luxuriant weeds.*

Hood, still unable to find a suitable place to bring Sherman to battle—at least where the odds would be in his favor—moved his army south to the town of Summerville before finally deciding to abandon Georgia and move into Alabama. Hood continued on to Jacksonville and then Gadsden to join Beauregard and be rejoined by the army's baggage trains and artillery. There, he was able to resupply his army with some of their needs—some getting shoes and clothing, and all getting a few days of much-needed rest.

Sherman had grudgingly followed Hood on what—in his mind—had amounted to a wild goose chase, but upon reaching the community of Gaylesville just inside Alabama, he halted his forces. Sherman was tired of the game and now wanted to go back to what he was planning—and trying to convince Grant to support—before Hood struck into his rear: a march to the Atlantic coast through Georgia.

Sherman took the step of sending Thomas to Nashville to gather forces there to watch Hood. He also let Thomas retain Maj. Gen. David S. Stanley's IV Corps and sent him Maj. Gen. John M. Schofield's XXIII Corps. Then, in an almost surreal event, Sherman took his army, turned his back on Hood, and went back to Atlanta.

Hood suddenly saw another opportunity. He would strike across the Tennessee River and hit at Sherman's supply lines in North Alabama. From there, he would move into Tennessee and make a rush for Nashville. In a meeting with Beauregard, the senior commander approved the plan.

Once again, the Army of Tennessee went forward—although, once again, without the bulk of its cavalry, which was ordered to move south to delay Sherman. Meanwhile, Maj. Gen. Nathan Bedford Forrest received orders to bring his command to replace Wheeler.

Destroying the railroads was, as one soldier recalled, a soldier's joy. Confederates did extensive damage to the railroad from Resaca to Dalton, but it ultimately proved to be only a mild inconvenience to Sherman. (cm)

The 24th South Carolina hastily built this line of limestone works at Shipp's Gap as Union forces approached from the east. (wlw)

Frustrated with Hood, Sherman gave up his pursuit near the Alabama state line and set a new target: the city of Savannah on the Georgia coast. (nps)

# A Slight Demonstration
## The Campaign through North Alabama

## CHAPTER FOUR
### *Late October-Mid November 1864*

Departing from Gadsden on October 22, Hood moved north over Sand Mountain, an area described by a Tennessean as "a dreary and desolate looking country." Then he moved on toward the Tennessee River and the town of Guntersville, where he planned to cross the Tennessee River. However, word came from the cavalry troops of Gen. Phillip Roddey, commander of the District of Northern Alabama, that Guntersville was strongly defended and had naval support, while Decatur, 40 miles further west, was only lightly guarded.

Concerned that Union gunboats might destroy his pontoon bridge, and being deficient of cavalry after the departure of Joe Wheeler's troopers—who'd been sent to oppose Sherman on his March to the Sea—Hood decided to make his way farther westward to Decatur, without letting Beauregard know of the change of plans. Decatur was situated on the south side of the Tennessee River with a Union pontoon bridge connecting it to the north side of the Tennessee. Hood hoped to use this point to cross his army over the river and then carry out his plan of moving into middle Tennessee.

Hood's forces arrived in Decatur, which was garrisoned by 1,800 men, on October 26. Decatur was heavily fortified by a line that arced around the town and secured itself on the banks of the river with forts at both ends of the arc. A line of abatis ran the length of the line with rifle pits in front. Any

Alabama was home to 31 infantry regiments, eight artillery batteries, and one cavalry regiment serving in Hood's army. A monument to the Alabamians, erected by the Sons of Confederate Veterans, overlooks the Franklin battlefield. (cm)

Gaylesville proved to be the end of the line for Sherman's pursuit of Hood. From here, Sherman moved back to Georgia—and ultimately to the sea. (wlw)

buildings outside the arc had been razed, providing a clear field of fire for nearly 1,000 yards. Adding to the defenses' strength, 17 cannon—a mix of rifled and smoothbore guns—were strategically placed around the town. The commander of the garrison, Col. Charles C. Doolittle, was—like all garrison commanders in North Alabama—on alert. He learned of Hood's approach when a cavalry patrol clashed with the Confederate vanguard.

When Hood reached the town, he ordered what he later called "a slight demonstration." His forces surrounded the town as best they could, and Doolittle withdrew all of his forces into the safety of their fortifications. Skirmishing and artillery fire marked the rest of the day.

As Hood's men worked through the night, Gen. Robert Granger, the commander of the Federal District of North Alabama, arrived to take over the Union defense. Having been alerted of Hood's arrival earlier by Doolittle, Granger sent word to George Thomas in Nashville that the whole Confederate army was before Decatur and that he desperately needed reinforcements. Thomas sent four regiments, one of which was the 14th USCT from Chattanooga, and the gunboat Stones River—along with orders for Granger to hold Decatur "at all costs." Together with the garrison already in the town, they brought the total strength of the force to around 3,000 men—no match for the 35,000-plus that Hood marshaled before them, although even Hood hesitated before the strong earthworks.

The next morning, the Confederates began to entrench and construct redoubts for their artillery

Signage in Cherokee County, Alabama, recounts the engagement near King's Hill Plantation described by William Stanard of the 103rd Illinois: "We were ordered out to rout some rebel cavalry that was bothering our outpost. We followed them about fifteen miles, routed them without the loss of a man, and then returned here again.... It seems we are doomed to march out the balance of our time." (wlw)

around the town, even as Hood inched his skirmishers closer and closer to the works. One of the defenders recalled, "We could hear the rebel pickets talking in an undertone within a stone's throw . . . ."

Heavy rain did nothing to help the situation. Confederate rifle pits and trenches soon flooded—in some cases with up to two feet of standing water. A heavy fog rolled in off the river, and the rattle of musketry soon echoed eerily all around the enshrouded town. Granger used the fog to his advantage and sent forward a series of small attacks that kept the Confederates at a distance and off balance.

**The weather turned foul as the Army of Tennessee advanced upon the Union defenses at Decatur.** (tya)

**This map from the Official Records of the War of the Rebellion Atlas displays the fortifications and the all-important crossings of the Tennessee River.** (or)

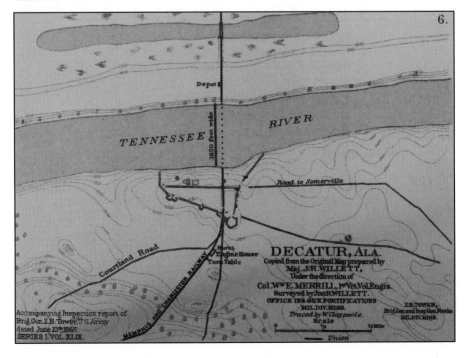

Gen. Robert S. Granger commanded the District of North Alabama and was on high alert as Hood moved westward from Gadsden. (loc)

On October 28, Granger launched several more determined efforts against the Confederate right and left. The attack on Hood's right was made by the 14th USCT, which rushed forward and overran four Confederate cannon with support from Union gunboats. "The order was at once given to charge . . ." Capt. Henry Romeyn of the 14th later wrote. "It required but little time to reach and go over the slight works, and driving off the artillerymen, spike the guns and get the prolonges down, to haul them off. But before they could be moved, the rebel Infantry had charged, and after a hand-to-hand fight the colored soldiers abandoned the attempt, and retired. . . . The charge and fight did not consume more than ten minutes . . . ." On their return to their works, they received hearty cheers from the rest of the garrison, which had witnessed their action.

Battle damage is still visible on the face of the Old State Bank, which was a short distance behind the Union defenses in 1864. (wlw)

More Union reinforcements soon arrived, bringing the garrison to nearly 5,000, and more cannon arrived, too. Coupled with the frustration of losing so much precious time, the reinforcements convinced Hood that the garrison couldn't be easily taken. Unwilling to launch a frontal attack against the fortifications, on October 29 he broke off contact and began moving his army westward, eventually marching 45 miles farther to the west. There, S. D. Lee's Corps launched a mini-amphibious operation and occupied the town of Florence, where they were welcomed as conquering heroes. Cheatham and Stewart moved a little farther to the town of Tuscumbia; here they went into camp, and the last soldiers from the 44th USCT were taken to repair the railroad that would soon supply the Confederate army.

The Army of Tennessee had made its most rigorous campaign of the war, and it showed. The men needed rest—as well as shoes, uniforms, and other necessities—if the campaign were to continue. Hood looked at his options and met again with Beauregard to outline a new plan: from Florence, he would move rapidly into middle Tennessee to strike at Nashville.

Beauregard approved, although he was frustrated that again he would have to oversee the logistics. After having established Gadsden as a supply base, the army was now more than 100 miles

**The Old State Bank is one of the only remaining witnesses to the fighting at Decatur. Today, a walking tour of the town starts at its location.** (wlw)

**Near this point, a pontoon bridge crossed over the Tennessee River. This was Hood's goal at Decatur. During the fighting, timely Union reinforcements arrived over this bridge, including the 14th USCT Infantry Regiment.** (wlw)

The scene of the charge of the 14th USCT as it appears today. "The conduct of the men on this occasion was most admirable," Col. Morgan recalled, "and drew forth high praise." (wlw)

Col. Thomas Morgan, a very proactive commander, led his 14th USCT into action at Decatur, having been rushed over from Chattanooga to aide in the town's defense. Morgan was soon promoted to command a brigade of USCT soldiers in the defense of Nashville. (chch)

west; Beauregard had to shift the supplies to this end of the state, which was no longer connected to any of the main Southern rail lines. He could get supplies as far as Cherokee, Alabama, but from there, it was a 15-mile haul over terrible roads to Tuscumbia. Adding to their woes, Hood now found a new enemy: Mother Nature, who proved to be his wily foe. A foul streak of heavy October rains raised the Tennessee above flood stage, making it impossible for Hood to have a pontoon bridge constructed to get Cheatham and Stewart to the north bank to join Lee.

Hood's forces endured a cold, miserable delay—one that ultimately lasted three weeks. It was precious time lost, as later events would show, though it did allow for Bedford Forrest to finally arrive with his mounted forces to restore Hood's cavalry arm to full strength, having had only "Red" Jackson's division since Wheeler's departure. Hood also tried to use the time to build a stockpile of rations—enough to last his men 20 days—but he was only able to accumulate seven days' worth before he was finally able to move north.

Hood's preparations and his restored cavalry, however, would not offset the mounting disadvantages caused by the delay. Not only was winter coming, but Thomas's strength was growing in middle Tennessee. Hood still had a chance, though, and he had better odds at this point than any other Confederate army in the field.

Hood launched an amphibious assault at Tuscumbia to take the north bank of the river at Florence, finally securing a place to cross the Tennessee. (b&l)

Markers like this guide visitors around downtown Decatur to the various points of the Union defenses and the actions that occurred there. (wlw)

*    *    *

When Sherman sent Schofield and Stanley with their corps to help Thomas deal with Hood, they went through a mini odyssey of their own. Stanley, via Chattanooga, made his way across North Alabama on the opposite bank from Hood and a couple of hard days' marches behind him. When he arrived in the town of Athens, he learned of Lee's occupation of Florence. Being at that time the only sizeable fighting force between Hood and Nashville, Stanley fell back across the Tennessee state line to the little town of Pulaski, marching into the town on November 4 and beginning to fortify a line of hills just north of the town. For the next ten days, Stanley and his men held a lonely and worrisome vigil.

Then, on November 14, elements of Schofield's XXIII Corps began to arrive, having been diverted to Johnsonville, Tennessee, a supply depot that had been captured and largely destroyed by Forrest on his raid. Schofield assumed command of the forces there plus some scattered cavalry—a total of around 26,000 men.

Schofield and Hood had known each other at West Point and been friends. Now Hood set his eyes on destroying his old friend's army—the only thing preventing him from moving onto Nashville and giving the Confederacy one last glimmer of hope.

## TENNESSEE, A GRAVE OR A FREE HOME

No words can describe the courage, endurance, and gallantry of the
Army of Tennessee. They marched, fought, bled, and died for a Cau
they knew was right. On that Indian Summer afternoon of Nove
30, 1864, the courageous Army of Tennessee deployed into
battle and marched over these open fields into immortal
memory of these heroic souls is as enduring as time. The
assured; it is only that of everlasting glory.

"A life given for one's country is never los
Sam Watkins, 1st Tennessee Infantry, C

# Tennessee: A Grave or a Free Home
## The March to Franklin Begins

## CHAPTER FIVE
### *November 21-29, 1864*

November 21 dawned bitterly cold as the last of Hood's troops made it to the north shore of the Tennessee River. "All the regimental commanders call their men out and say that Genl Hood says that we are going into Tenn. into the enemy's country, and we will leave our base of supplies here," recalled Capt. Samuel Foster of the 24th Texas Cavalry (Dismounted). "That we will have some hard marching and some fighting, but that he is not going to risk a chance for defeat in Tenn. That he will not fight in Tenn. unless he has an equal number of men and choice of the ground . . . ." Hood intimated that the men "would be short of rations" but that "he would do his best," Foster added.

With these words in mind, Hood's men began their march northward toward their date with destiny in Tennessee. Icy winds howled down from the North.

The beginning of the march proved to be a miserable experience. Willie Smith of the 48th Tennessee in Stewart's Corps noted in his diary, "Marched at sunrise—Snow, very cold. Ground frozen hard . . . icicles 2 feet long." For the next few days, the men marched through bitter cold.

Hood moved to outflank Schofield's position at Pulaski, with the hope of cutting him off and destroying him, and then moving on to deal with George Thomas. Hood decided that, to move faster, each corps of his army, preceded by cavalry troops,

A monument on Winstead Hill, on the edge of the Franklin battlefield, bears the prophetic words, "Tennessee: A Grave or a Free Home." The words were seen on a tarp that many of them marched under as they entered the state, which several Confederate soldiers later recounted, including Sam Watkins of the 1st Tennessee, author of the memoir *Co. Aytch.* (cm)

would move up a separate road to the west of Pulaski. The farthest column would be Frank Cheatham's, which moved up the road toward Waynesboro and then Mount Pleasant before turning east into Columbia; Stewart moved toward Lawrenceburg and nearest to Schofield; and S. D. Lee came up the middle along the worst road—all converging on Mount Pleasant and then Columbia. Holding Columbia was critical for Schofield. Located directly in his rear and bisected by the Duck River, the area was an essential crossing point for his army.

Sam Watkins, postwar author of the memoir *Co. Aytch* about his time in the 1st Tennessee, is buried in the cemetery of Zion Presbyterian Church outside of Columbia. (cm)

"Our progress was very slow," recalled a soldier in Cheatham's column, Sumner Cunningham. "The artillery and wagons cutting through mud to the hubs. Our impatience made the march seem very long. . . . As we approached the State line, we saw stretched out over the road a white strip of cloth about a yard wide and four yards long on which these words were boldly written: 'Tennessee's a grave or a free home.' The shouts and silent manifestation of joy and amen to the sentiment will never be forgotten . . . ."

In advance of all three columns, the cavalry ran into opposition from their Union counterparts. The cavalrymen would clash many times over the next few days, but the Union cavalry found itself overwhelmed and outmatched by Forrest's troopers.

By the afternoon of November 23, the Confederates were converging on Mount Pleasant and were within easy striking distance of Columbia. The weather was improving, entering a phase of Indian summer. "The glorious sun burst forth once more and assumed his rightfully supremacy, warming the blood, brightening all about us," a member of the famed 5th Company Washington Artillery noted. "It was manifestly the dawn of prosperity. Why not the dawn of victory? . . . Our advance was rapid not rash. Swiftly we pushed the enemy's columns before us. . . . There is nothing so heartens a man like an 'advance'. . . ."

Sherman sent Gen. John M. Schofield with his XXIII Corps to aide George Thomas in the defense of Tennessee. Schofield would experience a series of harrowing days as he tried to stay ahead of his old classmate, John Bell Hood. (loc)

Already uncomfortable in his post at Pulaski, Schofield received word from the Union cavalry that Hood was moving to outflank him and that the Federal cavalrymen were unable to arrest the advance. Schofield ordered his army to withdraw back toward Columbia.

Now it was a race.

Columbia was not without troops, but the

garrison wouldn't be enough if Hood got there first. Schofield ordered Gen. Jacob Cox of the XXIII Corps and Gen. George Wagner's Division of the IV Corps to rush northward. They arrived, in Cox's words, "just in time to interpose between our retreating cavalry . . . & the rebel Gen. Forrest, who was following them up sharply. . . . We were not a moment too soon." The unexpected appearance of the Union infantry ended Forrest's roughshod treatment of the Union cavalry for the moment.

Over these open fields, Union cavalry desperately tried to slow Nathan Bedford Forrest's advance on Columbia. (wlw)

The weather continued to grow milder as the Confederates moved into a region largely untouched by the blight of war. Soldiers were stunned to see plantations in their prime and to be cheered by locals. Many of the men's moods soared, while others remained grim.

Throughout the whole campaign, Pat Cleburne seemed to work under a dark cloud of foresight, and as the column approached Columbia, he took note of a beautiful Episcopal church. Marveling at St. John's, he drew up his horse before it for a moment, noting to one of his staff, "It is almost worth dying for to be buried in such a beautiful spot . . . ." But time was short for taking in the beauty, and Cleburne was soon moving on with his troops.

Both armies now began to arrive in the vicinity of Columbia, with Schofield's men constructing a strong line of entrenchments to oppose any further Confederate advance. Hood's veterans moved into line and began to entrench and martial their forces. By November 27, Schofield found his position in the town to be very tenuous. His back was against the Duck River. Reinforcements joined him. The two recently recruited regiments—the 44th Missouri and 183rd Ohio—would play an important role a few days later at Franklin, along with the 175th Ohio, which was a part of the town's garrison.

General James Wilson assumed command of all the Union cavalry opposing Hood. It took him some time to figure out how to deal with Forrest, though. (loc)

Also arriving on the march to Columbia was Maj. Gen. James H. Wilson, who arrived to take command of all of the scattered Union cavalry. That evening, he ordered his men to leave the town and occupy the

**Colonel Robert Beckham, chief of artillery for S.D. Lee's Corps, was mortally wounded on November 29th and buried at St. John's.** (wlw)

northern bank of the river. He hoped his new position would offer some natural defense from a frontal assault but also allow for a better reaction in case of another flanking movement—which was exactly what his old friend Hood was planning. "I determined not to attack them in their breastworks, if I could possibly avoid it, but to permit them to cross undisturbed . . ." he said. Hood intended to move rapidly, leaving the army's supply train, most of his artillery, and two of S. D. Lee's three infantry divisions in front of Columbia to draw Schofield's attention. The rest of the infantry and cavalry moved three miles eastward to cross the Duck River and, in Hood's words, "by a bold rapid march . . . gain the rear before he was fully appraised of my object. The situation presented an occasion for one of those interesting and beautiful moves upon the chess-board of war, to perform which I had often desired an opportunity."

Hood had tried a similar move the previous July in what became known as the battle of Atlanta, but the move failed due to a number of factors. Primarily, Hood's absence from that field prohibited him from dealing with a rapidly changing situation. This time he resolved to accompany the flanking column.

Their target would be the little community of Spring Hill, astride the Columbia Turnpike, approximately 11 miles in Schofield's rear. Hood wanted to catch Schofield between the two halves

**The timely arrival of Union infantry stopped Forrest's push on Columbia.** (tya)

Saint John's Episcopal Church, between Mount Pleasant and Columbia, stirred Patrick Cleburne's heart as he passed by. He noted that it was worth dying to be buried in such a spot. (cm)

of his army and crush him. It was a great plan if everything went right—but Lady Fortune had a bad habit of not smiling upon the Army of Tennessee.

Adding to the urgency of this, Hood received word when he arrived at Columbia on the 24th that Sherman was moving toward Savannah and would then move to reinforce Grant at Petersburg, putting Robert E. Lee's Army in a closing vice. "It is essential you should take offensive and crush enemy's force in Middle Tennessee as soon as practicable, to relieve Lee," warned Beauregard—but Hood needed no encouragement.

Forrest's cavalry moved out first. Spilling his troopers across the Duck at several locations, he drove back the Union cavalry—now all under Wilson's supervision—bringing darkness down over Schofield's "eyes and ears" at the critical moment. Confederate engineers went to work at Davis's Ford, constructing a pontoon bridge, and by the chill dawn of November 29, things were in motion for what would become one of the most debated and controversial episodes of the war.

# The Race to Spring Hill

## CHAPTER SIX
*November 28-29, 1864*

In his first outing against the man Sherman called "that Devil" Forrest, James Wilson found his horsemen steadily driven back by Forrest's. Wilson sent word to Schofield of this. Although he misinterpreted the Confederate's intention, expecting a move further to the East, his report still placed Schofield on the alert that something was up.

Cleburne's division led the way across the Duck and began making its way northward along the horrid Davis Ford Road. The road was a long-abandoned route defined by its rutted, overgrown, winding course, which forced some columns to move in nearby fields—which proved equally difficult due to muddy conditions.

Hood held some surprise over his old classmate, but Schofield remained leery. When word arrived of the Confederate crossing of the Duck, Schofield telegraphed Thomas, who sent word to withdraw Schofield's forces to the town of Franklin, about 12 miles to the north. Schofield began the movement by first ordering his wagon train onto the Columbia Turnpike along with the bulk of his artillery, with Brig. Gen. George Wagner's division as guards and under the supervision of General Stanley.

As both the Confederate and Union forces moved on their converging paths, the cavalry continued to clash. Forrest seemed to yet again have

Spring Hill offered Confederates one of their best opportunities of the campaign. (wlw)

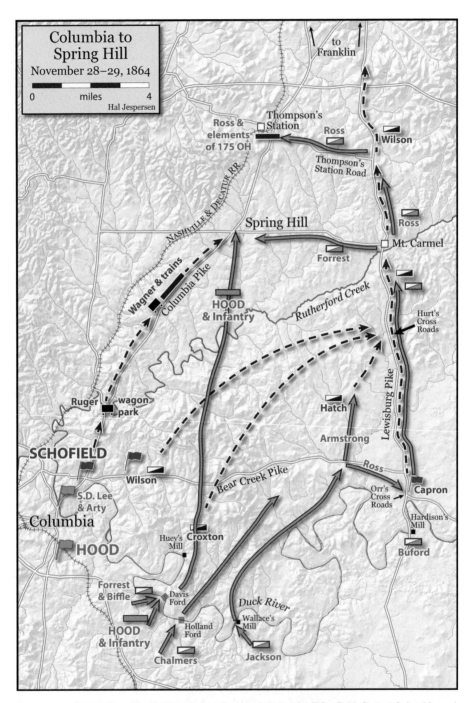

**COLUMBIA TO SPRING HILL**—Hood attempted to flank and then cut off Scofield, first at Columbia and then a few days later at Spring Hill. The march on Spring Hill failed in the twilight of November 29 when confusion, miscommunication, and insubordination let Schofield slip past the Confederate forces.

the upper hand as he continued to drive Wilson's troopers back from almost every point.

Then Forrest abruptly turned westward, moving rapidly toward Spring Hill on the Mount Carmel Road as Wilson continued his withdrawal toward Franklin. Around 11 a.m., Forrest's advance came into contact with the town's small garrison and other units drawn to the town's defense on the rolling hills just east of town. These men, armed with a mixture of different breech loaders and repeating carbines, slowed the Confederate thrust, which was already beginning to weaken because of the exhaustion of both men and animals. Forrest's troopers needed rest and ammunition after a day of nearly constant hit-and-run fighting, but Forrest remained aggressive as they neared the town around noon. The Union defenders quickly constructed a crude barricade of fence rails and other materials; lying down behind these works, they repulsed the Confederate advance.

At about the same time the vanguard of Stanley's troops began to arrive in sight of the town, Stanley received word from a courier about the Confederate presence. Stanley sprung into action and ordered Wagner to hurry his command forward at the double quick. Colonel Emerson Opdycke, in the lead of Wagner's column, moved through the sleepy little town at a run and positioned the column along a slight ridge just to the north side. The wagon train was arriving and moving into an open field near the town's train depot. Colonel John Lane's brigade was the next at the scene. Ordering the Spencer repeater-armed 28th Kentucky to lead

**Gen. Stephen D. Lee had the task of using his corps to hold Schofield's Federals in place.** (loc)

**The rest of Cheatham's Corps came up behind Cleburne. Bate would go into action in the distance.** (wlw)

Cleburne's brigades advance over this rise toward the Union positions. (wlw)

the way, Lane pushed eastward on Opdycke's right, driving back Forrest's dismounted troopers. "The enemy's cavalry charged . . . but was repulsed with loss," Wagner reported.

Brigadier General Luther Bradley's brigade arrived last and moved forward to occupy a hill on the southeast side of the village, disconnecting him from the rest of the Union line. He formed his men in an angle along the edge of the woods on the crest of the hill, and they began to entrench.

Forrest moved his force to reconnoiter to the south and soon came into contact with Bradley's skirmishers, who moved forward, "driving before it the cavalry, without replying to the harmless long range fire they kept up with their carbines." This prevented the Confederates from getting a clear picture of the Union position. Stanley, along with Wagner's men and the hodgepodge town garrison, had saved Spring Hill from Forrest—at least momentarily.

That was about to be put to the test.

*    *    *

Moving up the Rally Hill Turnpike, a long column of drab-colored men appeared bearing the distinctive blue banners of Patrick Cleburne's division. Hood's infantry was arriving on the scene with about an hour of daylight left. The march had been long and difficult, one of Granbury's Texans recalled, "On we went, through farms and by ways, over hills, through valleys and wading creeks as we came to them."

Now in sight of their destination, Hood told Cheatham to move his command to block the turnpike. Cheatham, in turn, told Cleburne to cooperate with Forrest and "take possession of and hold that pike at or near Spring Hill." Cleburne ordered his command to halt and form, facing toward the setting sun. He deployed his brigades en echelon, stepping from the Alabamians and Mississippians of Brig. Gen. Mark Lowrey's brigade on the right, to Brig. Gen. Daniel Govan's Arkansas Brigade in reserve in the center, and finally Brig. Gen. Hiram Granbury's Texans on the left. Forrest ordered one of his brigades, under Brig. Tyree Bell—which had earlier clashed with Bradley's skirmishers—to screen the Confederate advance on the right. But with only four rounds of ammunition left to each trooper, they would be of little service.

Cleburne ordered his command forward just a mile short of their objective: the Columbia Turnpike, which he was ordered to block by forming across it facing south. William Matthews in the 33rd Alabama of Lowrey's brigade noted, "about 4 p.m. advanced across a slope, across a field." As Cleburne's men moved westward, Gen. John C. Brown's division moved onto the scene, as well, but it was ordered to continue northward behind Cleburne.

As Cleburne advanced, Lowrey's flank began to move past Bradley's brigade, who "poured a deadly volley" into them. The blast of fire momentarily stunned Lowrey's men, forcing them to halt and turn north to face their assailant. Cleburne now had to halt his advance and order Govan's men to also move northward to face Bradley's men. Cleburne was heard to shout, "I'll charge them!"—and that's exactly what he did. While Granbury continued to move west toward the pike, Cleburne's division with their blue flags charged up the slopes into the Union line. Bradley's command was no match for Cleburne's veterans, and his troops were soon fleeing in disorder despite Bradley's attempts to rally them— up to the moment he was wounded. His men fled down the slopes and northward toward Spring Hill. Cleburne ordered his men forward in pursuit.

The chase soon came to an abrupt end. Gathered

Gen. David Stanley shone during his defense of Spring Hill—arguably his finest performance during the war. (tua)

Brown's Division moved up the Rally Hill Pike behind Cleburne's position. (wlw)

A native of Nashville, Gen. Benjamin Franklin Cheatham was known for his hard language and drinking and was very popular with the troops, especially those from Tennessee. (loc)

along the south side of the village, several Union IV Corps artillery batteries had arrived, placed by Stanley on the high ground. The guns opened fire upon the pursuing Confederates, staggering them to a halt. One exploding shell's shrapnel struck Cleburne's horse, sending the general sprawling, but it left him unhurt. Rising to his feet, he wisely ordered his command to withdraw and reorganize. He then sent a request to Cheatham for further instructions and support. It was now about 5 p.m., and darkness was settling over the field.

Brown's men continued past Cleburne's embattled troops, arriving in position a little further to the north. Accompanied by General Cheatham, who had been their longtime commander before promotion to corps command a few months earlier, Brown's men formed a line facing westward toward the southeastern corner of Spring Hill. Cheatham told Brown to launch an attack on the Union position east of the town once his division formed up. Once in position, Cheatham sent word for Cleburne to hold his position and wait for Brown to attack. For some reason, Cheatham had decided to attack the town and not simply block the Columbia Turnpike.

Meanwhile, Granbury found only one Union regiment and two cannon to oppose him, which he brushed aside. But he stopped short of the turnpike to reform with the rest of the division. Though he was unable to stop Cleburne, Bradley had diverted Cleburne from his task and prevented him from accomplishing his mission, which now fell to others.

*   *   *

The last of Cheatham's troops arriving on the field were Maj. Gen. William B. Bate's men. Bate's division formed south of Cleburne's initial line of advance and he moved his men forward en echelon toward the fading light of the sunset.

Bate's orders from Cheatham were to support Cleburne's left, but Cleburne was out of sight by the time Bate was ready to advance.

Then General Hood appeared.

Hood told Bate to advance to the turnpike and block it—the same directive given to Cleburne earlier. Bate moved forward over the rolling ground, still seeking to find Cleburne, when he heard the roar of gunfire from Cleburne's encounter to the north. Bate continued his movement to the west, but angled slightly to the north in an attempt still to follow his earlier orders of supporting Cleburne's flank, unaware that Cleburne was swinging his men further away.

**Cleburne's veterans pursued their opponents down this slope until halted by Union artillery fire.** (wlw)

As the field darkened with the 5 p.m. sunset, Bate approached the Columbia Turnpike, and now the sound of gunfire echoed through the dark. Bate's skirmishers found Union troops before them on the pike. They drove them off but then discovered a larger force was approaching from the south: Brig. Gen. Thomas Ruger's division, the

lead of Schofield's evacuating force. Bate gathered his officers to order them to move on the pike, but a courier from Cheatham arrived demanding that Bate move to the north to link up with Cleburne's left.

Bate was in a dilemma, so he held his position and sent to Cheatham for clarification. Meanwhile, Ruger's division continued up the pike. When Bate

**Just a short distance from their goal, Bate's Division was halted and then bivouacked for the night. After dark, the Union Army passed right by their campfires.** (wlw)

**Gen. John C. Brown became the source of much controversy over the years.** (nps)

finally got word back from Cheatham, it was short and curt: follow the order or report to Cheatham under arrest. Bate reluctantly gave up the ground and moved to form upon Cleburne's flank.

\* \* \*

In the growing darkness, Brown became nervous, and after advancing only 400 yards, he halted when he detected what he thought were Union soldiers on his right flank. At this time, Cheatham had returned to see why Brown had not opened fire yet. After hearing Brown's concerns, Cheatham rode off to see Hood and find out what could be done. Hood had made his way to a nearby mansion, Oaklawn, and established his headquarters there. Cheatham found him there. Over the next few hours, the headquarters would become the scene of some of the most controversial episodes of the Civil War.

Hood simply wanted an advance to block the road to prevent Schofield from escaping, but somehow that never happened—despite assurances that it was or would be done.

Darkness settled over the field, limiting Hood's options even further. He sent Lt. Gen. A. P. Stewart's arriving corps to cover Brown's left. Major General Edward "Old Alleghany" Johnson

**Hood made his headquarters at Oaklawn. During the night of November 29, Hood received reports and sent orders from here. When he finally bedded down for the evening, he thought he had Schofield trapped.** (wlw)

A Civil War Trails wayside tells the tale of the great opportunity Confederates lost at Spring Hill. (wlw)

also arrived with his division—the one division of Lee's Corps that brought up the rear of Hood's flanking column—and Johnson moved to the same point Bate had occupied earlier just north of the Rippavilla Plantation mansion.

There, Johnson saw opportunity. Years later, General S. D. Lee recalled to Hood "that Genl. Johnson did go to Genl. Cheatham and beg him to let him attack with his division, stating that he did not even require support, but that Cheatham refused, stating finally he was opposed to night attacks." Cheatham no doubt had in mind the blunder of a night attack he had been involved with at Chickamauga the year previous.

Here at Rippavilla, Hood took stock of the opportunity he lost the previous evening. (wlw)

All through the night, Schofield's army slipped past the Confederates, who finally went into bivouac just a few yards from the Columbia Turnpike. By dawn, the Federals—and the opportunity that Hood had worked so hard to achieve—had vanished.

Despite the finger pointing that ensued, the words of General Hood on the matter are best: "Thus the best move of my career as a soldier came to naught."

# At All Hazards
## The Union Forces Arrive and Deploy at Franklin

### CHAPTER SEVEN
*November 30, 1864–morning*

John Schofield rode up the Columbia Turnpike through the cold, starry night toward the little town of Franklin, Tennessee. Founded in 1799 and named for Benjamin Franklin, the town had boasted a population of 2,000 in 1860 before the war winds blew. "[T]he village came dimly into view as we marched northward," a soldier at the head of the army said. Schofield turned to Gen. Jacob Cox, commander of the lead division, and directed him to mass his troops "on both sides of the turnpike, leaving the way clear for the trains and let the men make their coffee . . ." Schofield then rode up ahead, arriving in the town around 4 or 5 a.m. on Wednesday, November 30.

Schofield was a very nervous man, but he was relieved to have escaped from the trap of Spring Hill. What he found once in Franklin, though, made that relief disappear like the morning mist. The town sat in a horseshoe-like bend in the Harpeth River, and Schofield hoped to find that a pontoon train had been sent there for him to bridge the river. However, the recent rains had caused the river to rise in its steep banks, sweeping away the bridges. The army would have to stay there until the bridges could be repaired—only then could they be back on the road to Nashville and safety.

Schofield rode south to confer once more with Cox. "I never saw him so manifestly disturbed . . ."

**Fort Granger remains a silent sentinel looking out over Franklin to this day.** (wlw)

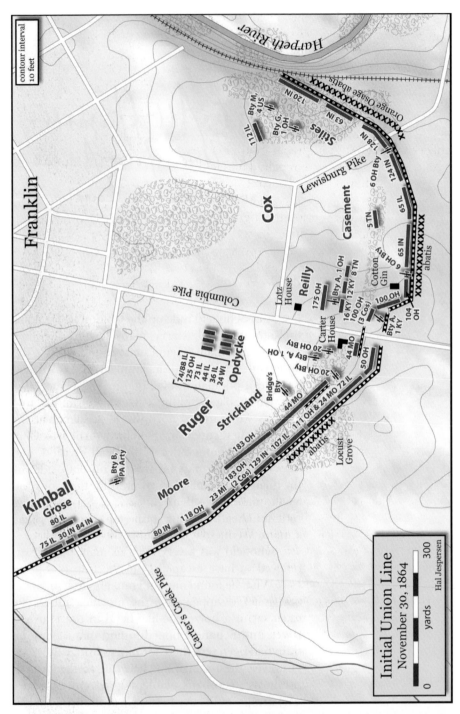

**INITIAL UNION LINE**—Arriving at Franklin on the morning of November 30, Schofield entrusted General Jacob Cox with preparing a defense of the town. Cox's masterful placement of troops and artillery paid great dividends later that afternoon when the Confederate forces attacked.

Cox remembered. "Pale and jaded from the long strain of the forty eight hours just past."

"General," Schofield told him, "the pontoons are not here, the county bridge is gone, and the ford is hardly passable. You must take command of the Twenty Third Corps and put it in position here to hold Hood back at all hazards till we get our trains over . . . ." He said Cox should let his trains and artillery move onward in preparation to cross over as soon as the bridges were repaired and added, "I will give you batteries of the Fourth Corps."

Jacob Cox made his way to the brick home of Fountain Branch Carter, located right beside the Columbia Turnpike as it made its way over a hill that bore the family name. Cox awoke the family and notified them that he would be using their home for his temporary headquarters until the crisis had passed.

Later, Cox would take the time to describe the battlefield from his position at the Carter house:

*Looking northward toward the town, a well marked slope leads to a lower level on which the place is built, the public square in its centre being forty feet lower than the knoll or bench at the Carter house. The pretty village itself is a third of a mile away, an open belt of fields and gardens then encircling it from river to river as it stands in the deep re-entrant angle of the Harpeth. The bend of the river is almost a right angle, and the stream washes the east and north sides of the town. As one goes up stream, he finds, after getting beyond the houses, that the valley turns to the southeast; but downstream it trends to the northwest, which is the general course of the river till it falls into the Cumberland, some thirty miles away. In the re-entrant angle the northerly bank is the commanding one, being not only of a higher general level, but having also well marked hills, on one of which (Figuer's Hill), enfilading the stream and railway on the eastern side of the village, was Fort Granger, a dismantled earthwork, built a year or two before. The railway bridge is perfectly covered by any artillery placed in the fort, and a deep cut in the railway at the edge of the town may also be thoroughly swept from that position.*

**Fountain and Polly Carter (top and above) lived in a one-and-a-half-story brick house Fountain built in 1830. Eight of their twelve children— including eldest son Moscow (below)—survived until adulthood. Another son, Tod, would be mortally wounded during the fighting at Franklin in what became one of the most famous stories of the battle. (bft)(bft)(bft)**

The railroad bridge over the Harpeth (bal)

Union Soldiers quickly went to work constructing fortifications around the south side of the town. (tya)

The selective placement of rifled cannon like this 3-inch ordinance rifle had devastating results on the attacking Confederates. (wlw)

*The streets in the town are not in the same direction as the turnpike at the Carter house. When the highway from Columbia enters the village, it turns to the right to reach a favorable place at the river for the bridge, and the squares are symmetrical with this line. The turnpike bridge had been destroyed early in the war, and had not been rebuilt. It was a single span of covered wooden truss, resting on high abutments. What was in 1864 known as the County Bridge was a lower and cheaper structure on trestles, built near the railway crossing, where a hollow on the north side made a practicable ascent for the roadway. This departure from the straight line of the turnpike added nearly half a mile to the length of the road, besides making it more difficult by reason of the grades. The ford was between the site of the former turnpike bridge and the county bridge. From the Carter house through the village to the ford is about a mile.*

*Turning now to the south, from the same point of view, it is seen that the Columbia Turnpike is nearly level, rising slightly till it crosses a low summit half a mile distant, and then dipping again so as to hide men or teams in the road. Most of the space to the Winstead Hill, two miles away, is so gently undulating as to look like a plain with a few depressions in it on right and left of the central ridge and road, where small watercourses run either way to the Harpeth. About half way to Winstead Hill, a bold, stony hill rises on the west of the turnpike, isolated in the general level around it, and known in the neighborhood as Privet Knob. Winstead Hill bounds the valley on the south, making part of a circle of ridges and heights, which seem to surround the basin in which the town lies. The Columbia Turnpike runs straight south, lost to view after it passes the low summit above mentioned, but coming into view again, climbing Winstead Hill by a white line rising from left to right, and passing over the crest between two of the rounded summits, which give the elevation a picturesque outline.*

*Two other turnpikes run from the town southward. That to Lewisburg goes up the Harpeth valley in a southeasterly direction. The other is at the west, and leaves the town by a similar angle. It is called the Carter's Creek Turnpike. The map of Franklin and its surroundings has been aptly compared to the left hand extended with separated fingers. The little finger and thumb at right angles represent the Harpeth River in its course from left to right, whilst the three fingers spread in the midst indicate the three turnpikes diverging southward from the village.*

*Half a mile southwest of the Carter house, and near the Carter's Creek Turnpike, is a hillock with a mansion and orchard known as the Bostick place. Between the two houses is a gentle hollow, which is about thirty feet below the level in the direct line from house to house. In it heads a small watercourse, which meanders through it, and, crossing the Carter's Creek Turnpike, curves northwardly to the Harpeth. This hollow, with its marshy brook, bounds the village on the west.*

**General Nathan Kimball served the first part of the war in the Eastern Theater before being promoted and transferred to the Western Theater in 1863. Kimball was noted for being involved in two early defeats of Robert E. Lee and Thomas "Stonewall" Jackson.** (loc)

*Looking eastward, the Carter Hill went forward a little, and one then saw, a hundred and twenty yards in front and eighty yards east of the turnpike, a cotton-gin, a strong frame building like a barn on the most advanced salient of the hill. To the left of this the ground descended a little, but rose again on reaching the Lewisburg Turnpike, half a mile away, where, between it and the railroad and a little in the rear, was another well marked knoll, through which the railway excavation cuts, as has been already mentioned. . . . Beyond the knoll and the railroad was the upper reach of the river, widening the field in front as it bore off to the eastward. Such was the field as it lay before us under the level beams of the rising sun. It was evident that the Carter Hill was the key to any strong system of defence in front of the town.*

\*    \*    \*

Opposite the Carter home, and about 150 yards to the southeast, stood the family's cotton gin, a 36-by-36 structure covered in weatherboarding on a stone foundation. General James Reilly, now temporarily commanding Cox's own division, moved off the Columbia Turnpike there and made his way east to form a line with his left resting near the Harpeth and then bending back to the west to the Columbia Turnpike. Engineer Levi Schofield recalled the deployment: "The Third Division of the Twenty Third Corps was led into position on the east side of the pike-Stiles, commanding Henderson's brigade, first, Casement next, and Reilly last, all facing the south."

Development eventually swallowed much of the Franklin battlefield, but as part of restoration efforts, preservations have been "uncovering" the battlefield. According to one estimate, modern streets cross former Federal earthworks in 11 places. For decades, only a single monument—erected in 1922 by the Tennessee Historical Commission—marked one of those spots. The monument still sits along U.S. 31 near Carter's Hill Park. (cm)

Next in line was Brig. Gen. Thomas Ruger's division, formed with his left near the turnpike and then running along the edge of the Carter property and down the slope of the hill to the west and bending back to the north as his right touched the Carter Creek Pike. When Brig. Gen. Nathan Kimball's division arrived in the van of the IV Corps, he moved behind Ruger to form to his left and extend his line back at a sharp angle to anchor his right on the Harpeth.

Once in position, the men stacked their arms, dropped their haversacks and knapsacks, and began to dig with a determination learned in the hard days of the Atlanta campaign. They strengthened their works with whatever they could find close by. The mulch from the weatherboarding of the cotton gin, farm equipment, outbuildings, and even railroad ties found their way into the soldiers' work.

They also utilized a couple of predisposed barriers. Along the Lewisburg pike there was a substantial line of Osage orange hedges—a tough, flexible, thorny bush used much like barbwire is today. It grew for some distance along the Turnpike, before turning west, parallel with the Union line. Soldiers went out and cut off the tops of the bushes, leaving the bottom half as a nearly impenetrable barrier; they then took the tops to part of the line without coverage and constructed a thick abatis by weaving the branches together.

On the western side of the Columbia

Turnpike, in the hollow below Carter House Hill, stood a grove of locust trees—another strong, thorn-covered tree that grew thickly. Soldiers cut some of the trees to again make an abatis, but they left others standing to serve as another natural barrier in the forthcoming fight.

Brigadier General Thomas J. Wood's division was told to continue up the turnpike and into town. Once the work on the bridge was completed, he moved his men to the north side of the river to be on watch in case Hood should try to flank the army again. As this went on, Schofield went back to the Harpeth crossings to oversee the work of his engineers repairing the bridge. He also sent orders to lay planking over the railroad bridge, so the army's wagons and artillery could cross more speedily.

General Thomas Ruger served though the summer of 1863 in the Eastern Theater, where, in his last service, he helped suppress the New York Draft Riots. In the Western Theater, he led a brigade in the XX Corps before being promoted to division command in the XXIII Corps. (loc)

As the IV Corps artillery arrived, its commander, Capt. Lyman Bridge, began to deploy his guns at intervals along and in support of the growing infantry line of defense. Some pieces stood on high ground behind the line to fire over the defending infantry; others were brought into the line itself, where gunners adjusted the earthworks by cutting embrasures into them, allowing the guns to shoot through.

Another deployment, although small, would have dire consequences for the Confederates: the occupation of Fort Granger by Capt. Giles Cockerill's Battery D, 1st Ohio Light Artillery. Fort Granger was a large, earthen complex built on Figure's Hill on the east side of town to protect the railroad bridge over the Harpeth in 1863. Cockerill placed his four three-inch ordinance rifles in the embrasures on the south side of the fort. With a commanding view of the river and the southeastern approaches to the town and the fields beyond, it was any artilleryman's dream—a virtually wide open shooting gallery to the maximum range of the guns.

General Jacob Cox would prove instrumental in the Union defense at Franklin. (nps)

The situation in the center, where the Columbia Turnpike entered the works, required special attention because the road needed to stay open so that the artillery and wagons could still pass through. To compensate for the required gap in the earthworks, a few yards behind the gap another line of works was built over the road—what was called

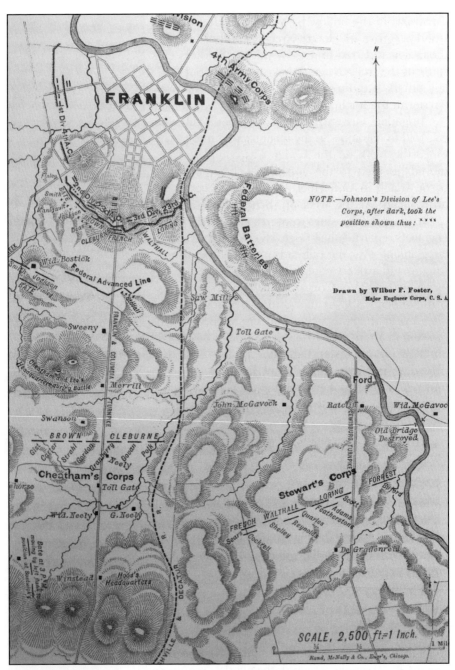

**A map from Jacob Cox's memoirs of the battle of Franklin not only shows the formation of the Union line, but also the terrain features that Cox recounts in his text.**
(baf)

a "retrenchment"—that ran on a line starting a few feet east of the turnpike then running across it and parallel with the Carter family's office and brick smoke house. Along this second line, one of the new recruit units, the 44th Missouri, occupied the Carter's yard with their line extending west. It was bookended by two sections of the Battery A, 1st Ohio artillery and the full battery of the 20th Ohio running along the line west of the smokehouse.

Where the prepared retrenchment ended, the line was picked up by the new recruits of the 183rd Ohio, who constructed a shallow line of works as the line sloped downhill to the west toward the Carter Creek Pike but ending before reaching it. East of the road, several regiments formed on the second line but did not entrench. Three regiments of Southern Unionists, Tennesseans, and Kentuckians, along with the new men of the 175th Ohio, would all soon play a critical role.

*　*　*

To the south, the rear guard of the army—Col. Opdycke's brigade—made its way wearily northward and deployed in a line of battle. Bedford Forrest's cavalry, "who kept popping away at us at every opportunity, without much, if any, effect except to waste ammunition," came nipping at the army's heels, remembered Adna Phelps of the 73rd Illinois. The morning alternated between sharp fights and retreats until the brigade reached the range of hills just south of the town around 11 a.m. There it rejoined the rest of Wagner's division, which finally halted two miles short of Franklin with orders from General Stanley to hold the line there and prepare breakfast. Opdycke was ordered to occupy the gap at the Columbia Turnpike and the eastern hilltop, known as Breezy Hill, while the rest of the division occupied the line further to the east and began preparing its breakfast.

On the opposite side of the pike, Gen. Walter Whitaker's brigade of Kimball's division was posted on Winstead Hill with two of his regiments in line of battle, while the rest of the brigade rested along the northern slope of the hill. Gunfire erupted from their line a little before noon when the Confederate cavalry made another probe. Whitaker ordered all of his regiments into line on the hill and soon was engaged. The fighting spread along the line to Opdycke's front as the Confederates developed the position, looking for

Among the soldiers to arrive to take position near the Cotton Gin was Harvey (above), the mascot of the 104th Ohio, the "Barking Dog Regiment." Harvey had been wounded at Kennesaw Mountain but Confederates returned him under a flag of truce. Harvey survived the war, and the Carter House now displays his collar, along with a small statue (below). (ch)(cm)

a weakness to exploit. But after about an hour, the cavalry broke off contact and withdrew.

As the fight ended, Whitaker received word to rejoin his division and departed the hill, leaving Opdycke once again as the sole rear guard of the army—although this time with the addition of a two-gun section of Battery M, 4th United States Artillery, which arrived during the skirmish with Forrest.

Wagner, seeing Whitaker's withdrawal, thought that he should also fall back, and soon his brigades were marching back toward Franklin. They did not get far before receiving orders from Stanley to "hold the heights you now occupy until dark, unless too severely pressed."

Opdycke was just beginning to make his way up the turnpike when he received his orders to turn back around and reoccupy Breezy Hill. But when they returned to their former position and looked south, they saw an ominous sight approaching: the van of Hood's army now appeared in two long columns. "In their butternut, clay colored clothing they looked like the sands of the seashore—and full as numerous," noted a member of the 125th Ohio—Opdycke's old regiment—nicknamed the Tigers. It was now obvious neither they nor the whole of Wagner's division could "hold the heights . . . until dark."

Opdycke sent word to Wagner, who was overseeing the placement of Lane's brigade on Winstead Hill, and Wagner lost no time in sending orders for the whole division to withdraw. He also sent word back to Stanley. By 1:30 p.m., Wagner was moving north with his men again.

As the column made its way toward town, they soon started over a little rock-strewn hill known as Privet Knob. Wagner decided to post Lane's brigade here with two guns of Battery G, 1st Ohio Light Artillery to act as a rear guard. Continuing on about a half mile to a swale across the pike with Opdycke's and Conrad's brigades, Wagner sent orders to Conrad to form another line by deploying his brigade in an open field to the left of the turnpike. Somehow, Wagner had decided that Stanley's orders still applied to hold a position in advance of the army—a critical mistake.

Wagner, seeing Opdycke approaching, rode over to him and told him to deploy his weary men on the western side of the road to extend the line. Opdycke had had enough, and with his temper about to boil over, he vehemently objected, pointing out that holding such a position would "aid the enemy and no one else," and that his brigade needed rest and food. So, he ignored the order and continued on toward town. An ugly scene played out as Wagner and Opdycke yelled and screamed at one another all the way to the Union main line where Wagner gave up, shouting, "Well Opdycke, fight when and where you damn please. We all know you'll fight." Opdycke continued on to a point just north of the Carter farm and finally his men were able to prepare their late breakfast and get some well-earned rest.

Opdycke deployed his men for rest on the long, sloping back side of the ridge upon which the Carter House stood. Not considered ideal at the time, their position would prove fortuitous once battle erupted. (cm)

Wagner stayed along the main line and made his way to the Carter House to meet with Cox, but still he remained convinced his advanced deployment was the correct decision. As he left the meeting, a courier from Colonel Lane galloped up to report that Confederate infantry was deploying in their front and would "swallow up his command." Wagner sent word for Lane to fall back to Conrad and establish his line to his right.

Wagner rode back to confer with Conrad, and, once there, told him "to hold the line as long as possible" and that the same would apply to Lane as well. To emphasize this, Wagner told Conrad "to have the sergeants fix bayonets and to keep the men to their places," then he once again rode back to the main line.

The seeds of disaster were being sewn in the old fields below Franklin. Wagner was making a terrible mistake.

# We Will Make the Fight

## Confederate Forces Arrive and Deploy

## CHAPTER EIGHT
*November 30, 1864–early afternoon*

A sense of disbelief, followed by anger, hung over many of the Confederates when they awoke in the frosty air. J. P. Cannon spoke for many when he wrote, "We were awakened before daylight and our mortification was even greater than it was last night to find that the game had flown; every one of them had 'walked right out of the trap.'" A Mississippian noted, "I have never seen more intense rage and profound disgust than was expressed by the weary, foot-sore, battle-torn Confederate soldiers when they discovered that their officers had allowed their prey to escape."

Hood also awoke to the stunning news. Despite multiple assurances from several of his commanders, none of them had managed to put any troops across the Columbia Turnpike—and Schofield had escaped. Hood was sure all was now lost. Schofield would make his way on to Nashville and join the force that Thomas was assembling there, and then things would get much harder to deal with.

Hood was angry and depressed.

Hood left Oaklawn and rode to the Rippavilla Plantation where he called some of his senior officers to meet him for breakfast. It was far from a pleasant meal. Hood is the only person known for sure to have been there, but most likely Cheatham and Stewart were present, as well. General Brown later told a staff officer that Hood "was wrathy as a rattlesnake, this morning, striking at everything." Whether his

Upon his arrival on the outskirts of Franklin, John Bell Hood surveyed the ground that would become the battlefield. Today, that location on Winstead Hill is now a memorial park, where a small pavilion offers visitors a sheltered opportunity to look over the same ground. (cm)

encounter was at the breakfast or afterwards isn't known.

Hood quickly had the army on the road toward Franklin in pursuit of Schofield. Stewart's Corps led, then Cheatham, and Lee once again brought up the rear, rejoined by Ed Johnson's division.

The march up the Columbia Turnpike brought some encouraging scenes to Hood's veterans. Debris of a retreating army seemed to be everywhere, along with many burned and abandoned army wagons. "The road was strewn everywhere with the wreck of thrown away stuff that they were unable to carry in their flight," observed Lt. Spencer Tally of the 28th Tennessee. Lieutenant William Berryhill of the 43rd Mississippi told his wife, "The road was strewn with tents, knapsacks, dirty clothing, books, papers, co. and regt. record books and c., and a great many wagons that they had cut the teams out and set the wagons on fire. I saw some wagons where they had killed the teams and left them. The women along the road appeared to be glad to see us and came to their gates and gave us bread and cheered us on."

By early afternoon, the hills south of the town

**Looking North from Winstead Hill over the open ground, largely fields in 1864, toward the Union lines.** (wlw)

of Franklin were beginning to loom in front of the gray column—along with the rear guard of the Union army posted on those same hills.

Forrest's cavalry led the Confederate pursuit, but by around noon, Stewart's infantry was on the scene, as well. With infantry to confront Wagner's rear guard, Forrest broke contact and moved with his forces to the east to join a brigade he had previously ordered to move up the Lewisburg Pike. At the beginning of the pursuit, he sent Maj. Gen. James Chalmers's division to push up the Carter's Creek Pike to the west. Stewart also received orders to move in that direction to flank the Union forces before them. The show of force led to the withdrawal of Wagner's rear guard sometime after 1 p.m.

Hood and some of his staff made their way to the top of Winstead Hill for a look at what lay before his army. What Hood saw must have brought a smile to his face: for the second time in 24 hours, a golden opportunity lay before him. Unexpectedly, he saw that Schofield was still there, which meant Hood still had time for one last attempt to eliminate his old classmate's army and give himself an unhindered approach to Nashville.

As Hood surveyed the Union line, he was joined by General Forrest, who reported that he thought the Union defenses were "exceedingly formidable."

"I do not think the Federals will stand strong pressure from the front," Hood replied to the dour cavalryman, "the show of force they are making is a feint in order to hold me back from a more vigorous pursuit."

"General Hood," Forrest countered, "if you will give me one strong division of infantry with my cavalry, I will agree to flank the Federals from their works in two hours time."

But Hood had made up his mind to try another tactic. The time for flanking was at an end. Though the Union forces were entrenched, he would order a frontal assault. His attempts at emulating Jackson at Chancellorsville had thus far failed, so now he decided on something different: a frontal assault similar to the one that had catapulted him to national recognition in 1862 at Gaines Mill.

With time and daylight running out, Hood would have to make the attack with what forces he could field at the time: Stewart's and Cheatham's

**The Harrison House.** (w/w)

corps and the handful of artillery present with them—
the bulk was with Lee's corps far to the south.

Although a frontal assault certainly appeared to be
a Hail Mary pass, it was really the only viable option in
Hood's mind. Thus far in the campaign, he had avoided
attacking strong entrenchments at Resaca and Decatur,
and he had tried but failed to flank Schofield at Columbia
and Spring Hill.

Hood stated with determination, "We will make the
fight."

\*    \*    \*

Hood sent word for his principle commanders to
come to him at the Harrison House a short distance
south of the hill range. Brown later noted that Cheatham
and Stewart were there along with himself, Cleburne,
and Bate. Forrest was still with Hood, as well, but no one
knows if any other commanders were present. Forrest
still disapproved of the attack, advocating for another
flanking movement. Cheatham and Cleburne, who had
both ridden to the tops of the hills before the meeting,
also expressed grave concern over making the attack.
Cleburne predicted the attack would be "a terrible and
useless waste of life."

General Brown recalled Hood's justification:

*"The country around Franklin for many miles is open and exposed to the full view of the Federal Army, and I cannot mask the movements of my troops so as to turn either flank of the enemy, and if I attempt it he will withdraw and precede me into Nashville. While his immediate center is very strong, his flanks are weak. Stewart's Corps is massed in McGavock's woods on the right, and I will send Bate's Division under cover of the hills to the left in advance of the movement of my center, giving him time sufficient to get into position to attack concurrently with the center column. He can connect with Chalmers's right . . . and with Brown's left. . . ."*

*He thereupon ordered Bate to move at once and directed Stewart to attack with his Corps the enemy's left flank. Cleburne and myself were directed to form in conjunction, Cleburne on the right and I on the left of the turnpike, and threaten and attack . . . the enemy's center, but were instructed not to move until further orders from him, as he desired Bate and Stewart, having a longer distance to march, to move in advance of us.*

Forrest was to have Chalmers's and Gen. Abraham Buford's divisions move on the flanks of the column—Buford on Stewart's right and Chalmers on Bate's left. Brown also noted that Hood did not ask for any further comments, and no one asked further questions. Hood was determined. He had

Cleburne gathered his brigade commanders on this hilltop to tell them the plan for the coming attack. (wlw)

tried everything else, so now, with the sun getting lower in the west and daylight fading, he ordered the attack.

As the meeting broke up, Hood spoke to Cleburne: "Form your division to the right of the pike, letting your left overlap the same," he told the division commander. "General Brown will form on the left with his right overlapping your left. I wish you to move on the enemy. Give orders to your men not to fire a gun until you run the Yankee skirmish line from behind the first line of works in your front, then press them and shoot them in their backs as they run to their main line, then charge the enemy's works. Franklin is the key to Nashville, and Nashville is the key to independence."

Cleburne mounted his horse and said in return, "General, I will take the works or fall in the effort."

\*  \*  \*

The commanders rode back to their commands to prepare for the coming assault. Cleburne called for his brigade commanders to meet with him on top of Breezy Hill where they would have a view of the ground over which their commands would soon cross. Years later, General Govan recalled Cleburne's explanation of Hood's plan: "He informed us that by the direction of Gen. Hood he had called everyone together to impress upon us the importance of carrying the works of the enemy at all hazards; that we were to move forward at the sound of the bugle, moving on the flank until we came under fire, then change front, form into line, fix bayonets and take the works at the point of the bayonet." Govan added that they "were further directed to have our field officers assemble, then our company officers, and issue to them similar orders."

The brigadiers descended the slope to meet with their regimental commanders and prepare them for the attack. As the meeting broke up, Govan recalled, "I saluted and bade him good-bye. I remarked, 'Well General, there will not be many of us that will get back to Arkansas,' to which he replied, 'Well, Govan, if we are to die, let us die like men.'"

Cleburne's and Brown's divisions now made their way over the crests to deploy at the foot of the hills,

**General Daniel C. Govan commanded the Arkansas Brigade of Cleburne's Division.** (loc)

Brown at Winstead and Cleburne at Breezy. One of Cheatham's staff, James D. Porter, remembered years later: "It was the grandest sight I ever saw when our army marched over the hill and reached the open field base. Each division unfolded itself into a single line of battle with as much steadiness as if forming for dress parade. . . . The men were tired, hungry, footsore, ragged, and many of them barefooted, but their spirit was admirable."

Meanwhile, a Union soldier on Wagner's line wrote more ominously: "A living wall of men and glistening steel was seen marching down the hillsides—filling the valley and sweeping across the fields. Close behind the first were other lines of troops; the whole pouring tumultuously onward, like the swift current of a river—bearing its burthen of seething waters resistlessly to the sea. At first the confused murmur of voices and martial music, like sighing breezes, filed the air . . . ." Another Union observer noted, "The rebels had filled the plain to the south, sounding to all like a tornado heralded by clouds of darkness and muttering thunders."

As the men moved into position, Cleburne rode out in front of the army to a little knoll where some of the army's deadly sharpshooters were practicing their trade on Wagner's line and the adjoining Union skirmish lines. There he dismounted and "remarked that he had left his field glasses behind and that he wished the use of telescope. Lieutenant Ozanne . . . quickly detached the long telescope from his

**Cleburne's Brigades formed up along the east side of the Columbia Turnpike in a column of brigades.** (wlw)

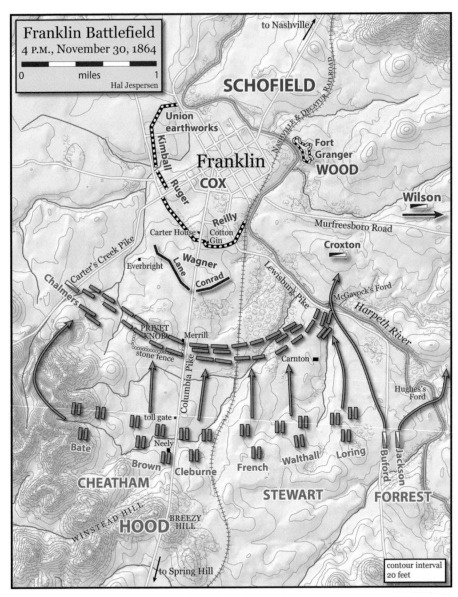

**FRANKLIN BATTLEFIELD—The Army of Tennessee formed up in the plain before Franklin while Forrest's cavalry corps split to cover both flanks. The few artillery batteries with the army were sprinkled throughout the attack force.**

gun, adjusted the focus, and handed it to General Cleburne, who laid the telescope across a stump and looked long and careful over the field, and remarked, 'They have three lines of works,' and then, sweeping the field again as if to make himself certain, said, 'and they are all completed.'" He then returned the telescope, thanked Ozanne for its use, and with fiery eye and rapid movement mounted his horse and rode rapidly to where his division was forming.

Cleburne went on to meet Hood again, asking permission to form his division in a column of

**The sun going down over the fields of Franklin on the 150th Anniversary of the attack.** (wlw)

brigades, which Hood granted. Meanwhile, the troops continued to move into position. The rest of the army's divisions adopted a formation of two brigades in front and either one or two in reserve, with the exception of French's undersized division, which now only fielded two brigades.

All were now tense in the army; all waited for the signal to go.

Along the Union line, a young man in the 104th Ohio, posted right in front of the Carter family's cotton gin, observed his surroundings: "Brother John is a few steps away, staring out over the breastworks as if in trance," he noted. "Far to the south, I hear a band. . . . Looking around at the different boys, I see Willie crying. I am told he received word of the dying of his only daughter by small pox. . . . I heard Captain Bard say to Lieut. Reed 'Do you think the Lord will be with us this day?' Silently, I said a prayer. Some of the boys shook hands with our Captain. The air is hazy, I can hear bands playing, and I see a few Rebels being deployed in a line of Battle in the far distance."

*It Seemed to Me that the Air was All Red and Blue*

*The Missouri Brigade Attacks*

## CHAPTER NINE
*November 30, 1864–4:40 p.m.*

Samuel French brought the army's smallest division forward onto the field. He moved them from the Lawrenceburg Pike westward toward the setting sun and formed them just to the left of the Nashville and Decatur Railroad's dirt embankment—the first Confederates to form on the field. On the other side, a half-mile away, Cleburne's men began to march onto the field and into their columns for the advance beside the Columbia Turnpike.

French was down to two brigades—his small Texas brigade was left to guard the army's pontoon train when Hood advanced into Tennessee, leaving him with Sears's Mississippians and Cockrell's elite Missourians. However, the aftermath of Allatoona was still being keenly felt: Cockrell mustered only about 700 men for his entire brigade.

French formed his command into a simple column, with Sears deploying his men in front and with Cockrell in their immediate rear in reserve. "The sun was sinking in the west, the day was drawing to its close, the tumult and excitement had ceased," French recalled. "The winds were in their caves, the silence that precedes the storm was felt; the calm before the earthquake which by some law of nature forewarns fowls to seek the fields, birds to fly away, and cattle to run to the hills, although withheld from man, seemed to presage an impending calamity . . ."

The tension was palatable, but not to the point that humor couldn't be found by the hardened

One hundred and thirty members of the Missouri Brigade are buried in the Carnton Cemetery. (wlw)

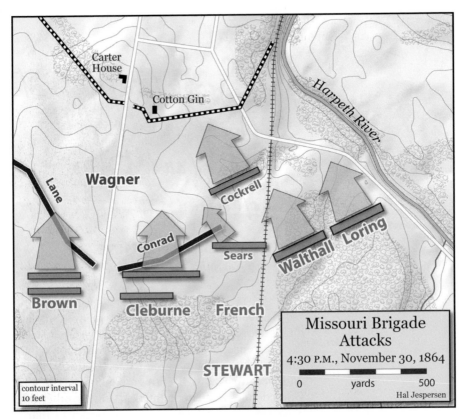

**MISSOURI BRIGADE ATTACKS—** One of the most storied commands in the war's western theater, the Missouri Brigade forever sealed their fame with their assault at Franklin. By a stroke of bad luck, they struck the Union defenses first, alone, and unsupported. The brigade seemed to melt away in the eruption of cannon and rifle fire.

veterans of the 1st Missouri Infantry, made up largely of Irish immigrants from St. Louis. "England expects everyone to do his duty!" said one soldier, quoting Lord Nelson before the battle of Trafalgar. One of the Irishmen replied, "Its damn little duty England will get out of this Irish Crowd!" Captain Boyce remembered, "The laugh . . . raised on this was long and hearty . . . laughing in the face of death."

Other distractions followed. Colonel Gates drilled his regiment, and the brigade band began to play its tunes, but as the rest of the army finally came onto the field, General Cockrell learned what was expected of them. He rode to the front of his men and told them what was to come, finally saying, "I'll lead the charge."

When the order to advance was received, Cockrell bellowed, "Shoulder Arms! Right Shoulder Shift Arms! Brigade Forward! Guide Centre! Music! Quick time! MARCH!" Sears did the same for his Mississippians a few yards to their front. The brigades stepped forward as the band struck up "The Bonnie Blue Flag," and moved forward with them. "It was an unusual thing for the 'tooters' to go up in a charge with the 'shooters,'" Captain Boyce recalled.

*   *   *

Two corps of the Army of Tennessee moved forward in unison. Even the Union main line watched in admiration. Levi Schofield later remembered the scene:

> *It was a grand sight such as would make a lifelong impression on the mind of any man who could see such a resistless, well coordinated charge. For the moment we were spellbound with admiration, although they were our hated foes; and we knew that in a few brief moments as soon as they had reached firing distance, all that orderly grandeur would be changed to bleeding, writhing confusion, and that thousands of these valorous men of the South, with their chivalric officers, would pour out their life's blood on the fair fields in front of us.*

French shared that sense of awe. "It was a glorious and imposing sight," he wrote, "and one so seldom witnessed, as all were in full view." William Kavenaugh attested, "Never in all our history had we gone into battle with better discipline or prouder step."

The pageantry didn't last long. The whirring sound of incoming artillery shells joined the music of the bands and the tramping of thousands of feet. Explosions rained hot iron down upon the heads and shoulders of some unfortunates.

Sears and Cockrell moved forward over the railroad, and soon Sears's left became engaged with the flank of Conrad's brigade in their exposed position. This slowed the brigade at first, then brought it to a halt. The Missourians kept going, passing the Mississippians and continuing on toward the Union main line. The "advance was general," one Missourian recalled, "and the line moved forward with banners streaming and the band of our Brigade playing. . . . [T]he line, in solid and unbroken ranks, charged on."

A deadly situation was now developing for Cockrell's men. With Sears falling behind and with Cheatham's corps confronting Wagner's line, the

A monument to the Missouri Brigade stands among the collection of memorials on Winstead Hill. (wlw)

General Francis Marion Cockrell commanded the famed Missouri Brigade. He later wrote, "At Allatoona, GA., I lost one-third of the number taken into the fight, and at Franklin, Tenn., I lost two-thirds—having had every fourth man killed dead, or mortally wounded, and since died. This was by far the fiercest and bloodiest and hottest battle I have ever been in." (mo)

**The Missouri Brigade raced ahead of the army, directly toward the Union line east of the Columbia Turnpike and in front of the Carter Cotton Gin—an imposing structure visible above the line of earthworks.** (bal)

left flank of the Missourians was now uncovered. To their right, the same thing developed as Walthall's division began to lag behind. The Missourians were on a course to hit the main line first—and alone.

As they came closer to the Union line, the blue artillery picked up its work, sending men sprawling, wounded or killed by the hot iron—and the worst was yet to come. Ahead of them, Union infantry brought their weapons to bear, aiming them and waiting.

*   *   *

To their front, the men of Col. John Stephen Casement's brigade had been distracted by the whole spectacle before them: the advance of the army, Wagner's stand, and now, through it all, the rapidly approaching Missourians. Jack Casement was standing upon the works, surveying the chaos. Noticing the Confederates, he turned to his men and shouted, "Men, do you see those damn rebel sons of bitches coming? . . . Well, I want you to stand here like rocks, and whip hell out of them." The plucky colonel then turned to face the charging Confederates once more and emptied his revolver into the onrushing horde before prudently jumping back into the trenches and moving to his post behind the line.

Nearby, the 65th Illinois Infantry—also known as the "Second Scottish Regiment"—prepared to open fire. A number of its members sported Henry repeaters, and for the second time in less than two months, the Missourians would feel the fury of being

under the fire of repeating weapons. Within a few moments, men all along the line were taking aim at Cockrell's men from in front and on both flanks. The honor of being the first brigade to strike the Union position was going to carry a heavy cost.

Archeologists uncovered the remains of the foundation of the Carter family's Cotton Gin. (cm)

When the Union line erupted with an unbent fury of artillery and gunfire, the Missourians seemed to melt away like ice before a blazing sun. "It seemed to me that the air was all red and blue, with shells and bullets screeching and howling everywhere, over and through us, as we rushed across the cotton fields strewn with fallen men," remembered Capt. James Synnamon of the 6th Missouri. Officers and men crumbled at an alarming rate. General Cockrell came crashing hard to the ground as his horse was shot out from under him. He managed to clamber to his feet while a staff officer dismounted and handed him his own horse, which Cockrell quickly mounted and moved forward.

It was a scene of unparalleled death and destruction as the very air seemed alive with lead and iron.

A multitude of scenes now played out as one of the premier fighting units of the Confederate

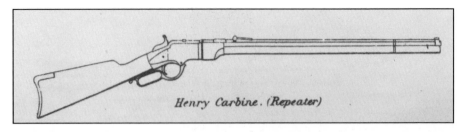

Henry Carbine. (Repeater)

**For the second time in the campaign, the Missouri Brigade had the misfortune of clashing with men armed with Henry repeating rifles.** (or)

army experienced its death throes. One soldier remembered, "In less than half a minute half of them went down."

Cockrell, waving his sword and screaming loudly in a futile effort to be heard above the maelstrom, was struck three times and fell heavily to the ground, wounded. His staff fared the same, all falling wounded or killed. Command of the brigade now passed to Col. Hugh Garland, desperately

pushing his regiment forward while holding the regimental flag in one hand; and then he was mortally wounded.

Irish-born Capt. Patrick Canniff miraculously remained mounted as he tried to hold his 3rd and 5th Missouri (Consolidated) Regiment together as they pushed onward. In a moment of desperation, he spurred his horse

**In this vicinity, the Missouri Brigade seemed to evaporate under a hurricane of fire. The lines of gravel mark the Union entrenchments.** (wlw)

forward at the blazing Union works alone. Several Union officers, admiring his courage, tried to keep their men from shooting him, but it proved in vain. Only 30 feet from the works, Canniff pitched backward off his horse with a wound to the shoulder. On the ground, he tried to rise up only to be struck fatally in the face.

Colonel Elijah Gates, the last standing commander, pushed his men onto the breastworks, where he was struck at close range by several shots that broke both of his arms and tore apart his uniform.

The survivors now hit the works, many jumping into the outer ditch and pressing against the earthen wall for safety, while others jumped over and

A reclaimed portion of the battlefield around the Carter Cotton Gin offers a peaceful view of the center of the storm. (cm)

clambered up the works in a futile attempt to break the line. Many were shot down or bayoneted and rolled back into the ditch, dead or wounded. Still others pitched over among the defending blue coats, and others were dragged over as prisoners of war. A few made a rush back to the rear in an attempt to find safety.

What remained of the gray brigade now endured a hellish experience as some men tried to continue the fight from the ditch, attempting to return fire in the growing darkness. They were soon joined by some of Sears's Mississippians and other troops as the rest of the army finally caught up with them—but little was left of the Missourians. The few minutes of undistracted attention from the Union line had virtually destroyed them as a fighting force. "The little amount that was left was wiped off the face of the earth . . ." one Missourian, B.F. Murdock later lamented.

The destruction of many more storied units of the Army of Tennessee was just beginning.

### Maj. Gen. William W. Loring's Division

During the Battle of Franklin this Confederate division, composed of three brigades commanded by Brig. Gens. Winfield Scott Featherston, Thomas Moore Scott, and John Adams, swept past Carnton as it approached the Federal line just after 4 p.m. on November 30, 1864. Subjected to artillery fire in this area, Loring's Mississippi, Alabama, and Louisiana troops took casualties with each step as they closed upon the Federal works. Carnton was quickly taken over as Loring's field hospital and the first wounded were taken into the house around sunset. By the time the battle ended around 9 p.m. Gen. Adams was dead, Gen. Scott was wounded, seven of Loring's sixteen regimental commanders were wounded or dying, and nearly 1,000 of his 3,500 men were casualties. Today, many of these fallen soldiers rest in the nearby McGavock Confederate Cemetery.

# Run Against a Chinese Wall
## Walthall and Loring

## CHAPTER TEN
*November 30, 1864–4:35 p.m.*

Stewart's Confederate corps made its way around the southern edge of Breezy Hill along a little farm lane then onto the Lawrenceburg Pike. It began moving northward before halting and deploying in the woods just south of the sprawling MacGavock plantation, "Carnton." Stewart formed with Gen. William Loring's division on the right and Gen. Edward Walthall's in the center and General French's reduced division on the left near the Nashville and Decatur Railroad—altogether around 8,000 men. The ground in front was a mixture of flat open fields and some wooded areas, but also it had a rolling nature with a series of dips and swales that ran parallel to the fields and outbuildings of the plantation as the ground neared Franklin to the north.

Walthall deployed his division with his left beside Sears's brigade of French's division. He deployed two brigades in his front line: Brig. Gen. William Andrew Quarles's Tennessee and Alabama brigade on the left and Brig. Gen. Charles Shelly's Alabama and Mississippi brigade on the right. Brigadier General Daniel H. Reynolds's Arkansas brigade made up the reserve behind Shelly.

To the right of Walthall, Loring posted his command with Brig. Gen. Winfield Scott Featherston's Mississippians on the division left and Brig. Gen. Thomas Scott's Alabamans and Louisianans on the right, joined by the line of dismounted cavalrymen of Buford's division. Their

A marker tells the story of the advance of Loring's men through the fields around the Carnton plantation. (wlw)

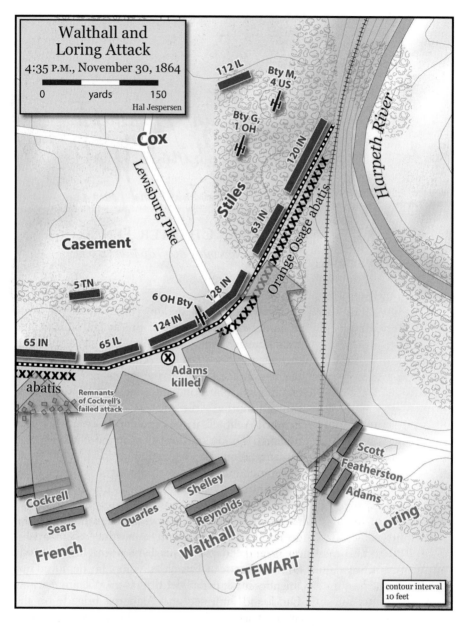

**Walthall and Loring Attack**

4:35 P.M., November 30, 1864

0    yards    150

Hal Jespersen

Cox

Harpeth River

112 IL

Bty M, 4 US

Bty G, 1 OH

120 IN

Lewisburg Pike

Stiles

Casement

63 IN

Orange Osage abatis

5 TN

128 IN

6 OH Bty

124 IN

65 IN    65 IL

Adams killed

abatis

Remnants of Cockrell's failed attack

Scott

Featherston

Adams

Shelley

Cockrell

Quarles    Reynolds

Loring

Sears

French    Walthall

STEWART

contour interval 10 feet

**Walthall and Loring Attack—** The bulk of A.P. Stewart's Corps advanced through the grounds of the impressive Carnton Plantation—passing through the Southern dream and into a nightmarish hell of death and destruction along the Union left.

reserve line was the large Mississippi brigade of Brig. Gen. John Adams. Adams's brigade had escaped some of the bloodletting of the previous campaign and came onto the field with nearly twice as many men as its sister brigades.

Walthall and Loring formed in open woods just south of the sprawling Carnton Plantation. For these men—survivors of the siege of Vicksburg and the struggle for Atlanta—the scene before them

presented an almost surreal quality. They were about to advance over ground that represented the pinnacle of Old South society—indeed, the ultimate dream.

Stewart received word from Hood via a staff officer to move forward, and orders soon made their way down the chain of command and the gray ranks began to move forward. As they emerged from the woods and clambered over a fence and into the open fields around the plantation, it wasn't long before men heard the distant boom of cannon and then the screech of an incoming shell, followed by the inevitable blast overhead. Positioned upon a low ridge behind the Union line to their front, six rifled cannon opened fire as Stewart's men moved into the open fields near Carnton. "We had not gone far before the artillery opened on us," wrote Capt. Joseph N. Thompson of the 35th Alabama of Scott's brigade. "Their first shot struck one hundred yards in our front, their second went over us and the third burst just above our Regiment, and I remember casting my eyes down the Reg. and seeing almost the entire right bow to it—after that they had found the range and almost every shot left a gap in our lines . . . ."

Another officer in Adams's brigade recalled that the "first fire struck my regiment, killing and wounding seven in Company 'I'. . . . We advanced through a clump of woods, the artillery all the time playing on our advance column, cutting limbs from the surrounding trees. . . ."

This was the beginning of an unrelenting storm of lead and iron that pelted the Confederates as they made their way forward, leaving a scattered trail

**John and Carrie McGavock (above and top) owned Carnton. In 1860, the plantation had 39 enslaved people working the fields. The Battle of Franklin Trust has worked to tell a fuller story of the Carton plantation, including interpretation that commemorates the forgotten lives of Carnton's enslaved people.(above left).** (fbt)(fbt)(cm)

**General Edward C. Walthall was slightly wounded at Franklin. He also had two horses shot from under him during the assault.** (bal)

of dead and wounded in their wake, in what one Tennessean called "a fine opportunity of testing their skill at long range."

Walthall soon encountered trouble of another kind. Reynolds's advance came upon some rough broken ground that was choked with thick, tangled underbrush, slowing the brigade to a crawl. Walthall halted Quarles and rushed Shelly's men to take Reynolds's place to keep the advance going. Unfortunately for French's division to their left, this uncovered their flank as they kept advancing.

Walthall's men now moved forward with a determined step over the rolling fields toward the awaiting blue infantry behind their works. "Both Officers and men seemed fully alive to the importance of beating the enemy here at all costs, and the line moved steadily forward," Walthall later recalled. They quickly came under fire of the Union skirmishers of Casement's brigade, who fired a few shots and then began their own hurried withdrawal back to the protection of their fortifications.

As the Confederates closed in on these fortifications, they crossed over the railroad embankment of the Nashville and Decatur Railroad. There, the fire of the 12-pound Napoleon smoothbore mingled with the blasts of the rifled cannon. Closer yet to the fortifications, the seething blast of small arms fire interspersed by shotgun-like blasts of canister from other cannon along the lines also pelted the advancing butternut brigades.

Through it all, the men struggled forward, following their colors as shells began to rip and tatter those banners, in what John Copp of the 49th Tennessee termed a "hurricane of combustibles" that left "ruin and desolation in its pathway." Walthall reported that his advance "was done under the most deadly fire of both small arms and artillery that I have ever seen troops subjected to. Terribly torn at every step by an oblique fire from a battery advantageously posted at the enemy's left, no less than by the destructive fire in front, the line moved on. . . ."

Out of the smoke that seemed to enshroud the last few yards in front of the blazing Union line, a member of the 1st Alabama of Quarles's brigade recalled "friend could not be distinguished from foe at a distance of a few steps. . . . Through a dense smoke and tempest of iron, our officers still leading, and the rebel yell still ringing, the army . . . charged. . . ."

That rush soon came to a staggering halt because a new threat emerged. Heretofore unseen was the line of abatis made from the Osage orange tops. "The abatis was most elaborate," a Confederate staff officer attested, "the boughs of the Osage hedge being interlocked; while the sharpened planks, sloped so as to strike the breast were set deep in the ground, nailed to crosspieces, It was impossible to get through this hedge, and our heaviest loss was occasioned while our men were trying to pull away the abatis. . . ." But this did not stop men from trying. Officers leapt forward and began to hack at it with their swords. Others tried desperately to bash it with the butts of their muskets or wade into it only to find themselves caught in the entanglement. All their efforts proved what one Alabaman later reported was an obstacle that "no organized force could go" through. All the while, blasts of gunfire tore through their ranks as men swore, screamed, cried, and shouted—combining with the rebel yell, the noise created a cacophony of hell that was noted even among the roar of battle, described by one of Quarles's men as "so rapid that it was impossible to discover any interval between their discharges."

**A thick line of abattis like this one proved to be a fatal barrier that made it impossible for many Confederate soldiers to even come close to the Union line.** (or)

With Quarles caught in front of the abatis, Casemates poured an unrelenting fire of repeaters and muskets into them. Despite this, the Confederates made some breaks in the abatis line. Among them was Colonel Shelley, now on foot after his horse was killed under him, who encouraged a handful of men and was finally joined by others able to find a way through the thorny abatis. With a shout, they lunged forward toward their tormentors, their momentum carrying them to the works—in some cases to the top of the works. "They leaped down into the ditch, climbed up the embankment enveloped in a sheet of fire, and from the ramparts discharged their pieces in the face of the enemy, and with butts of guns closed in a hand to hand grapple with the foe," wrote Edward McMorries of the 1st Alabama.

Casualties fell at an enormous rate. General Quarles fell with a grievous wound to his head, and all of his staff was dead.

John Copp of the 49th Tennessee found "two large army pistols" on the body of a dead Union soldier in front of the ditch. "I quickly removed them . . ." he wrote, "and with one in each hand emptied them under the head logs at the mass of men across the works in my front."

Savagery became the rule as the Union line proved unbreakable in this sector. Though mounting the works and planting their flags, the Confederates got nowhere. Others—seeing the futility of it—broke to find cover that might be afforded by the lower ground to their rear.

Through the mass of fugitives, coming up from reserve, Reynolds's Arkansans added their weight to the attack. "When aboute 100 yds of their works our men opened fire and rushed like Demons on to their works," an officer in the 4th Arkansas recalled. "We found the Ditch on the out side and went in it, nothing between the two armies in Deadly Combat but a huge pile of Dirt. Numbers of our men climed on top of the works to be instantly Killed or mortally wounded. We Kept up a heavy Fire over the works in to their men who was Massed behind the works."

Reynolds himself noted, "I never saw my brigade in finer trim, and when they met the retreating mass they cheered and tried to induce them to return, moving on steadily until within some 15 or 20 steps of main line . . . here the fire became so terrible that we were forced to fall back . . . we fell back some 1,000 yards and collected the men. . . ."

General John Adams commanded one of the largest brigades in the Army of Tennessee because it had been spared some of the bloody fighting during the Atlanta Campaign. (cmh)

To their right, things weren't going much better for Loring's division. Loring's men advanced around Carnton, streaming over its fences and around the mansion itself before moving on toward the Union line. They found themselves being pushed westward as the Harpeth's angling course guided them toward the narrow Union front. Loring's men began moving forward at the double quick as more and more artillery shells began to pound their lines. As they

One of the most storied incidents of the battle of Franklin was the death of General Adams and his horse upon the Union works near the Cotton Gin. (bal)

General William W. Loring was known for his profanity—so much so that he was nicknamed "Old Blizzards" due to the storm of oaths he was known to unleash. (loc)

closed toward the main line, long-range shots from the guns in Fort Granger began to strike into Scott's brigade on the end of the formation.

Advancing Confederates moved up and down in wave-like undulations as the ground funneled toward the Harpeth, but ahead of them, as they neared the railroad, the ground rose steadily toward the Union line. Some found the Osage orange hedge that had provided the abatis that caused so much trouble for Walthall. The hedge was planted in a v-like formation along the western side of the railroad as it ran north into town, and then it angled back toward the Lewisburg Pike. Scott's and Featherston's men rushed into it and became ensnarled. Federals "opened terrifick fire of shot, shell, grape, and cannister," a lieutenant in the 43rd Mississippi later wrote his wife, "and when the troops got to within 400 yds. the musketry united with cannon and it appeared to come by the millions. I cannot see how any human being could live 2 minutes in such a place. Our Division got to within a few steps of the works and some went upon them. Others could not get there for a thick hedge row of thorn bushes . . . ."

Colonel Marcus D. L. Stephens and others of the 31st Mississippi made it through. "We reached the railroad and pressed on through the thick mat of thorn bushes. . . ." he reported.

Along these quiet streets, thousands of A.P. Stewart's men struggled to reach the Union defenses in the waning daylight of November 30, 1864. (wlw)

*We had worked our way through this thorny obstruction, under a heavy fire and formed in front of it when the order was given to fix bayonets and charge. . . . Our Color Sergeant, with the flag, was by my side when the order came. All of the Color Guard, nine in number, had been shot. As the bearer fell in the desperate charge, he handed me the flag. I took it with misgivings, feeling that I would be shot, but I could not refuse to take it. I, with the flag in my hand, rushed to the breastworks to plant our flag on their works.*

**Loring's men moved through the fields at Carnton under a murderous artillery fire, then moved over this rise as they closed in on the Union lines.** (wlw)

Stephens—like many others—didn't make it all the way: he fell wounded.

All along the line, similar events occurred. The Osage orange wreaked great havoc in the face of sheets of Union fire. One officer in the 128th Indiana faced the onslaught and noted that, as he ordered his men to open fire, Confederates

*never flinched; but defiantly moved on until they struck the hedge, where they were balked as completely as through they had run against a Chinese wall. They made desperate efforts to penetrate it without avail. Human nature couldn't stand the destructive fire that was rained upon them, and they began to move quickly by the flank so as to pass around the hedge. When they reached the road they tried to force an entrance through the brush that had been cut down. Seeing their exertions, I directed the fire of two companies full upon them right down the road, and they were compelled to flank again. Having passed the brush they came back in one grand rush . . . one color bearer sprang upon the works and was instantly shot. . . . Another color bearer was shot in front of companies A and F . . . Their field officers and several captains were either killed or wounded, and they broke and fled in confusion. It was a terrible assault, and most terribly was it punished.*

**Today a trail lets visitors follow part of the advance of Scott's Brigade of Loring's Division through the fields at Carnton.** (wlw)

Some of Loring's men attempted to crawl down the railroad using the cut and embankment for cover, but fire raked them down their flank. Soon those who

**A historic marker marks the scene of the fighting on the Confederate right.** (wlw)

were not trapped in the ditch were running for the rear. As they streamed out of the smoke, Loring rode among them, trying to rally them. Chaplain James McNeilly of Quarles's brigade witnessed the scene: "As they streamed back General Loring was riding among them. . . . He was commanding, exhorting, entreating, denouncing . . . but to no purpose, for the bullets were flying thick over and among them. . . . General Loring . . . turned his horse to face the enemy. . . . He sat perfectly motionless, with his sword . . . lifted high above his head . . . and cried out in anguish; 'Great God! Do I command cowards?' Then he galloped after them. . . ."

Loring's men were far from cowards this day, but they had suffered tremendously. Still, he had one more part of his command to go in: John Adams's Mississippians.

Adams, astride his horse "Old Charley," brought his brigade forward. It was twice as large as Loring's two front-line regiments. As the Mississippians navigated their course across the battlefield, the men shifted westward toward the roaring fight around the Cotton Gin, where Cleburne's men had recently struck. Adams was wounded—shot in the arm—but kept on. "I am going to see my men through," he told one of his staff.

Once again, Casement's men unleashed hell into the onrushing gray mass. Casualties mounted with every step forward. Part of Adams's line struck the abatis, and that familiar story was repeated again, though at least one soldier came prepared: Private Wesley Peacock of the 15th Mississippi sported an axe, and he "ran forward and began to cut away the hedge and continued doing so until he saw his company falling back, and strange to record, he came out untouched."

Others found their way clear, moving over the same ground that was littered with dead and wounded remains of the Missouri brigade. Momentum built as they came closer to the lines. Seeing his men begin to falter in the face of the scathing fire, Adams set spurs to his horse and galloped toward the Union entrenchments. Casement and others were stunned by this display, but it ended in a blast of fire just as "Old Charley" brought Adams right to the very edge of the Federal line. Horse and rider fell, riddled dead with bullets. A few of Adams's men also made it to the works but were unable to break through—the line here was simply too strong for mortal men to overcome.

Stewart's attack had lost many of his best men. Generals Scott and Quarles were wounded, Adams lay dead at the very edge of the Federal entrenchments, and many other field and line officers were gone. In Quarles's brigade, the highest-ranking officer left was a captain.

General Thomas Scott was severely wounded by the concussion from an exploding shell as he led his brigade through withering fire along the Lewisburg Pike. (cmh)

Sunset from the fields near Carnton. (wlw)

# THE COTTON GIN ASSAULT

Into this area rushed elements of four Confederate divisions on November 30, 1864 as they assaulted the Federal line near the Carter cotton gin. Crossed largely by troops from Maj. Gen. Patrick Cleburne's Division, the area was also flooded by men from Maj. Gen. Samuel French's Division, and some from Maj. Gen. John Brown's and Maj. Gen. Edward Walthall's divisions. The Southern troops charged forward, crashing into the section of the Federal line between Columbia Pike and the gin held by Brig. Gen. James Reilly's Brigade. Two pieces of Ohio artillery just to the north, near the cotton gin, inflicted horrific Confederate losses. Yet the assault led by Cleburne's troops broke the Federal line and vicious hand-to-hand fighting erupted.

CITY OF FRANKLIN

# The Ferocity of Demons
## Cleburne and Brown

### CHAPTER ELEVEN
*NOVEMBER 30, 1864—4:45 P.M.*

They each considered themselves to be the best in the army, the very heart and soul of the Army of Tennessee from its inception just before the battle of Shiloh, although it was called the Army of Mississippi at the time: Patrick Cleburne and John C. Brown. Ironically, though, facing the Carter home was the first time their two divisions formed to go into battle together, side by side.

Cleburne's division formed upon the east side of the Columbia Turnpike with Govan's Arkansans in front, then Granbury's Texans, and finally Lowrey's Mississippians, all with their distinctive blue banners flying—the last vestiges of the famed Hardee Corps battle flag that had become the hallmark of Cleburne's command. Across the turnpike, Brown deployed his men in a "two up, two back" formation, with Brig. Gen. States Rights Gist's brigade on the front left—the only brigade in the whole division not made up of Tennesseans, with men hailing from South Carolina and Georgia. Next was Brig. Gen. George W. Gordon's brigade, and in support behind Gordon was Brig. Gen. Otho F. Strahl's command. Beside him and behind Gist was Brig. Gen. John Carter's brigade.

As the men waited and some bands played "Dixie" in Brown's division and "Bonnie Blue Flag" in Cleburne's, some officers made last-minute preparations while others gave speeches and instructions. No one doubted the gravity of the attack they were about to make, especially Cleburne.

Four Confederate divisions assaulted the area around the Cotton Gin. A state historical marker recounts their story.
(cm)

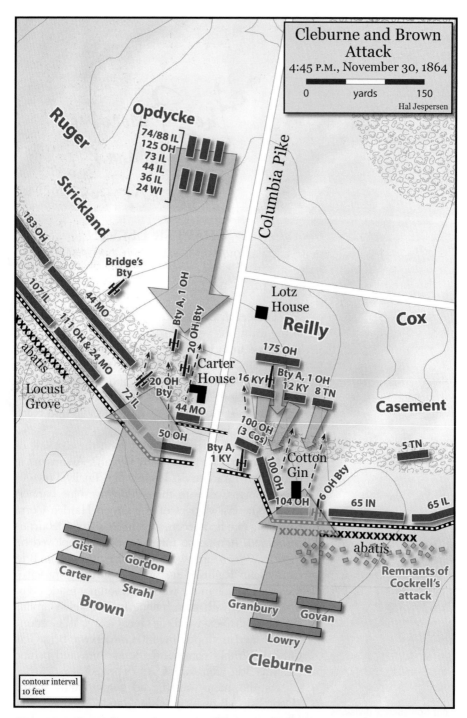

**Cleburne and Brown Attack**—As veterans of every major battle, Cleburne's and Brown's divisions made up the heart and soul of the Army of Tennessee. Formed up along either side of the Columbia Turnpike, their desperate assault actually carried them over and through the Union defenses, but Union reserves stopped them.

A soldier in the 1st Arkansas later watched his commander prowl: "Genl Cleburne rode along our line said boys save your ammunitions. You must use the bayonette. . . ." Other commanders gave more patriotic speeches or tried their best to prepare their men, although General Strahl offered only a simple caution: "Boys, this will be short, but desperate."

In Strahl's front, George Gordon pointed across the turnpike to Granbury's Texans. He reminded his men that they were "Tennesseans on Tennessee soil and we must not suffer ourselves to be outdone this day even by such gallant fighters as the Texas Brigade."

Cheatham told his commanders that the signal for the attack would be the dropping of a flag, and at 4 p.m., the flag fell. All along the lines, a flurry of activity erupted as bugles blared, drums beat, bands began to play, and officers bellowed the orders. Then both divisions moved forward. Cheatham later noted they "were steady as a clock."

"It was the most impressive movement I ever saw," one of Govan's staff officers, George A. Williams remembered, "the Grey line moving gradually on with blue & red colors dancing above, like a wave" rolling toward Wagner's ill-placed brigades.

Conrad's and Lane's men worked furiously to entrench, using their bayonets, cups, plates, and bare hands to excavate as much dirt as they could and put it between them and the forming lines of the Army of Tennessee. Then a hint of movement caught their eyes. Some stared while others were startled by the low rumble of the sound of thousands of marching feet. The time for entrenching had passed, and men cast aside their cups and plates and grabbed their weapons. Seeing the tidal wave of gray and brown headed toward them, some of General Wagner's men began to curse and plead. Others demanded to be allowed to fall back to the main line before it was too late.

The Confederate line swept down into a low swale, and as it emerged, cannon boomed from behind Wagner's line, sending howling shells downrange into Cleburne's division, where the shells exploded. The 1st Kentucky Battery, along the main line manning rifled guns, had just inflicted the first casualties of the assault. The section of artillery posted at the apex of Wagner's line also opened

General Patrick R. Cleburne, born in County Cork, Ireland, to a prominent Protestant family, immigrated to the United States after a short stint in the British Army. Cleburne rose from private to major general in the Army of Tennessee, but due to his nativity and a lack of a West Point education, his advancement ended there, though he was one of the best division commanders in Confederate service. (loc)

fire at the approaching Confederates, firing rapidly round after round down the turnpike, switching from shells to canister as the distance closed.

This support gave little consolation to Conrad's and Lane's men. "Nearer and nearer the Confederates approached with the precision of dress parade, and our hearts beat rapidly," one soldier recalled.

**The men of Lane's brigade entrenched as best they could in the fields that extended to the west toward the Everbright Plantation.** (wlw)

Finally the guns were ordered to limber up and make their way to the rear, leaving the infantry to their own devices. A staff officer from Wagner galloped up to Conrad and, as Conrad later remembered, announced,

*the general ordered that, if the enemy came on me too strong and in such force as to overpower me, I should retire my line to the rear of the main line of works . . . but, as the enemy was so close to me, and as one half of my men were recruits and drafted men, and knowing that if I then retired my line my men would become very unsteady and confused, and perhaps panic stricken. I concluded to fight on the line where I then was. So I ordered the men to commence firing.*

A blast of musketry issued from Conrad's and Lane's infantry as the Confederates halted and adjusted their lines. Then the bugles blared and officers ordered their men to advance at the double quick. One Ohioan noted that the Confederates "appeared a solid human wave. . . ."

*It was a grand sight! Such as would make a lifelong impression on the mind of any man who would*

**The approach to Privet Knob from the point of view of Cleburne's left flank.** (wlw)

*see such a resistless, well conducted charge. For the moment we were spellbound. . . . As forerunners well in advance could be seen a line of wild rabbits, bounding along for a few leaps, and then they would stop and look back and listen, but scamper off again, as though convinced that this was the most impenetrable line of beaters . . . that had ever given them chase; and quails by the thousands in coveys here and there would rise and settle, and rise again to the warm sunlight that called them back. . . . They rose high in the air and whirred off to the gray sky light of the north.*

The fire of Wagner's men staggered the Confederates for a moment, although some of them also returned fire. For a brief time, the two lines blazed away, and then orders came down along the Confederate line to charge. "Soon as we came in range," a lieutenant in the 5th Arkansas recalled,

**General George Wagner's placement of his brigades in front of the main Union line nearly proved to be a fatal blunder and became a source of great controversy for a man who prior to those events was a proven commander in the Army of the Cumberland. (loc)**

*the Yankees opened fire on us from behind their entrenchments and were first killing and wounding our men. My color bearer was shot and the flag fell across my pathway. I picked the flag up and as I unfurled it to the breeze, Col. P. V. Greene . . . who had gone into the fight on foot grasped the flag staff and said in his familiar way, 'Damn! I'll carry the flag—look after your own company.' . . . They were killing and wounding our men so fast . . . the order charge was given. We raised the Rebel Yell and moved in quick time but before we reached the works the Yankees fled in disorder. Our boys emptied their loaded guns into the confused ranks of the fleeing troops. . . . I noticed General Cleburne. . . . The gallant old hero with hat in hand and waving it above his head scaled the works from which we had routed the Yankees. I could not hear what he was saying but knew he meant to go forward. Again we raised the 'Rebel Yell' and renewed the charge. . . .*

Conrad and Lane did all that could be expected. They resisted for a few moments, but with pressure along their entire front and with both flanks now being turned, their line gave way and the men began to run back toward the safety of their main line, 800 yards away. Utter chaos developed as Cleburne's and Brown's men came hot on their heels, shooting, stabbing, clubbing, and even tackling the retreating

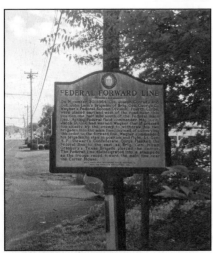

**A modern view south from the site of Wagner's advanced line overlooks urban sprawl; on November 30, 1864, the men of Cleburne's and Brown's divisions filled this area.** (wlw)

foes. The chase was now on and a cacophony of shouts was now raised as the Tennessee rebel yell mingled with the cheer of South Carolina and the more primitive shouts of the Texans and Arkansans. The two forces soon became intermingled as it became "Devil take the hindmost."

General Gordon, who went into the attack on foot, like quite a few others, years later spoke of those moments: "When they fled the shout was raised by some one of the charging Confederates; 'Go in the works with them! Go into the works with them!', This cry was quickly caught up and wildly vociferated from a thousand straining throats as we rushed on after the flying forces we had routed-killing some in our running fire, capturing others who were slow of foot, and sustaining but little loss ourselves. . . ."

Ahead of the surging horde, soldiers along the Federal main line looked at the mob with rapidly growing concern. If they fired, they would mow down many of their own men, but if they didn't act quickly enough, they would soon find themselves locked in hand-to-hand struggle with some of the best troops in the Confederacy. Foot by foot, the mob of blue and gray approached. The more fleet-footed of Wagner's men clambered over the works, followed by the bulk of the gasping blue wave that came over the works. Moment by moment, more and more came over—with the Confederates rushing ever closer.

An enlisted man beside the turnpike described the scene: "Rebel Flags and Union Flags were fluttering in the breeze; rebel officers were waving their swords and calling their men to come on. Away on our left the ball had already opened; the crash of musketry and boom of artillery and the bursting of shells could plainly be heard above the yelling of the hordes in our front. . . ." Finally, the moment of no return arrived: either open fire or have the Confederates overrun the line. Despite the fact that some of their own men remained in front, Cox's line opened fire.

General Gordon was just a few feet west of the Columbia Turnpike, "within a hundred paces of their main line and stronghold, when it seemed to me that hell itself exploded in our faces," he later recalled. "It yet seems a mystery and a wonder how any of us ever reached the works alive." Men fell all around the general, but as one Tennessean recounted, others scrambled forward. "Our lines had become broken," he said, "and the men rushed onward regardless of order, converging toward the pike till they became solid masses, all anxious to reach . . . the breastworks."

**The ground between Wagner's line and the main line at the Carter Farm became a scene of panic and chaos as Confederates overwhelmed Conrad's and Lane's brigades after the Federals made a strong but futile stand. (wlw)**

Reaching the Federal position, the Confederates jumped over the ditch and clambered up the sides and into a brutal melee. The lines of regiments and brigades melded together into a mob as they pushed over the works where they could and moved forward.

The battle now reached a point where the outcome seemed to hang in the balance. Hood's men breached the center of the Union defenses and began making a hole about 200 yards wide. If they could keep widening it and thus penetrate further, their assault just might work—now was their chance.

The 50th Ohio fell back through the Carter family's garden. Holding for a little while longer on the front line, the 72nd Illinois finally gave way, too. Captain James Sexton said, "The 50th Ohio on our immediate left was swept away in the first mad rush, the enemy occupying part of their works. . . . [H]ere for a time we were badly intermingled, many of the men using the bayonet and others the clubbed musket; every officer was busy with his revolver." But Confederates finally forced Sexton's men back through the Carter garden, too. The Illinoisans jumped over the works and joined the 44th Missouri, who had also been joined by some of Wagner's men.

Together, the combined force hefted their weapons and opened fire, turning the area between the two lines of works into a slaughter pen. "The crashes of musketry exceeded any that I had heard in front of Atlanta," said Erastus Winters of the 50th Ohio, who had taken cover in the floor of the front line trench among dead and wounded Confederates.

As the Tennesseans pushed on into the Carter

A series of tablets along a walking trail near the Carter House visitor center tell the story of the Confederate breakthrough. (cm)

BROWN'S DIVISION
ARMY OF TENNESSEE
C.S.A.

yard—through a hurricane of lead that ripped and tore them—they met the green soldiers of the 44th, who now proved their worth by resisting the engulfing tide. Using the Von Clausewitz maxim that the best defense is a good offense, Colonel Robert Bradshaw ordered his Missourians to take the initiative and charge. They drove the Confederates back to the outside of the first line of works before falling back to their own Union defenses. Twice they executed this tactic, buying time and unbalancing the charging Confederates, who were then joined by Strahl's brigade from the reserve. This added more impetus to yet another, albeit weaker, Confederate attack across against the Carter's yard. Parts of the Federal line did sway back, and some Federals broke, while others rallied and returned to the fight. In the end, the second line would not yield, delivering "a deadly hair of minie balls" into the Confederates.

Lieutenant Edwin Reynolds of the 5th Tennessee later recalled how the attacks weakened and finally ended. "The bravest spirits crossed the entrenchment and advanced a few yards, but finding themselves almost surrounded by Federals . . . . They retired behind the entrenchment, but kept up a fire on the enemy. In vain did the officers urge the men on to cross the breastworks; they were too nearly exhausted and the fire was too deadly even for the bravest to face."

\*   \*   \*

As Gordon pushed his Tennesseans on through the deadly hailstorm of lead toward the works on the turnpike, Hiram Granbury shouted to his Texans "Never let it be said that Texans lagged

in the fight!" in a bid to outrun them. But the general suddenly jerked, threw his hands to his face, and fell to his knees as his men surged around him. Struck in the head, Granbury was dead.

**Brown's men burst over the second line and around the outbuildings at the Carter House.** (wlw)

"This advance and charge came nearer measuring up to the pictures of battle we see in the books than anything we saw during the war," one Texas officer said—but it was at a terrible cost.

Amidst it all, Cleburne urged his men on, dashing his horse among them. Then his horse was shot down "not 50 yards from the breastwork . . ." said Govan, witnessing the event. "Then his courier brought a fresh horse [but] a cannon ball . . . struck him and tore him in two. Just as horse was killed in the smoke & confusion he waved his cap over his head-50 yds from pike-50 yds from works & then waved the men forward." Govan lost sight of Cleburne then, the "fire so heavy & smoke so thick could not see 20 steps ahead."

The Texans and Arkansans struck the line in front of the Cotton Gin. Those close to the pike went over the works and captured the guns of the 1st Kentucky Battery, driving back their supports: the 100th Ohio Infantry and a few companies of the 104th Ohio positioned in front of the Cotton Gin. Through a knock-down, drag-out brawl, the line held. Wiley Washburn, a member of the 1st Arkansas said, "I gone out of the ditch and was on the side of the works, at the SW of a gin house, but mercy, the

**Advancing on foot, General Hiram B. Granbury urged his men onward along the Columbia Pike shouting, "Never let it be said that Texans lag in a fight." Those were his last words.** (loc)

Over this ground, Cleburne and many of his men took their final steps as twilight fell across the battlefield. (wlw)

In this vicinity, the 1st Kentucky Battery blasted cannister into the onrushing Confederates in a final act of defiance before being overrun by Cleburne's veterans. (wlw)

yanks that were there. . . . I raised my gun to get my man and was shot in the right elbow, my hat shot off, my gun stock broken with 100 holes thru my blanket. So I laid down in the ditch. They began a cross fire on us and were doing us lots and lots of harm." Indeed one Union soldier later testified, "I never saw men in such a terrible position as Cleburne's Division was in for a few minutes. The wonder is that any of them escaped death or capture."

Lowrey's men pushed into the fight. Year's later, Lowrey called it "the most destructive fire I ever witnessed." In recounting the events, he said, "I threw my brigade into the outside ditch of his massive works and my men fought the enemy across the parapet. Up to this time about half of my men had fallen, and the balance could not scale the works. It would have been certain death or capture to every one of them."

"The enemy's loss was awful," one member of

the 104th said. "You can have no idea of it unless you could see the field. The nearest fighting in our Brigade line was directly in front of our Co. We were the left center Co., next to the Colors, and they seemed determined to capture them, but our boys stuck to them. The rebels came up on to our works, some of them jumping clear over them. The ditch in front was piled with dead and wounded and for rods in front, a man could hardly put his foot down without stepping on them."

Most of the 104th held their posts in a savage fight accompanied by the sounds of their mascot, Harvey, who gave the unit its nickname, "The Barking Dog Regiment."

Some of Cleburne's men spilled around to the west and moved forward like Gordon's men on the opposite side of the turnpike. Ahead of them also lay a line of Federal reserves: the 8th Tennessee, the 12th and 16th Kentucky, and the 175th Ohio, plus two guns of Battery A, 1st Ohio Light Artillery. Levi Schofield later described it thus: "Now was the great opportunity for the brave Cols. Rousseau and White and the battery commander, Charley Scoville," Levi Schofield later wrote.

Like his neighbors, the Carters, woodworker Johann Albert Lotz—who lived in this house—found his home in the whirlwind of war. After the battle, it was said, there was a carpet of bodies from the house, across the turnpike, to the Carter House. (wlw)

*The two former were in command of Reilly's second line and had been cautioned by Gen. Cox . . . to look out for a break at this point, and when it did come they were ready. . . . They did not wait for an order, but sprang over the low rifle pits like tigers, and with a shrill shout that was heard even above the rebel yell, and heroism rarely equaled by men, went pell-mell into the mass of Confederates that had taken our line, and did not know what to do with it. At the same time Charley Scoville cracked his blacksnake whip about the ears of his artillerymen, and drove them back to the guns. At it they went with pick-axes and shovels, slashing all around them with the ferocity of demons.*

Again, vicious hand-to-hand fighting raged along the line as Cleburne's men tried in vain to overcome this last line of defenders.

As the roar of battle escalated between the Carters' gin and home, Col. Emerson Opdycke had his men up. He had received word from Cox

General Emerson Opdycke's arrival at Franklin was a bit of a homecoming. In the first half of 1863, Opdycke and his newly formed regiment, the 125th Ohio, were assigned to garrison the town. Opdycke and the veterans of the 125th returned on November 30—not to garrison, but to fight. (loc)

Opdycke's men streamed over this ground and into the Carter House yard, where they slammed into Brown's and Cleburne's men in a vicious close-quarters fight in the gathering darkness. (wlw)

a short time earlier to get his men ready and was in the process of forming his brigade on the east side of the turnpike when the cacophony of the fighting erupted in their front. Men from Wagner's command fell back, with their commander trying to rally them, along with some of the unnerved green troops of the 44th Missouri. Overwhelmed by the tide, Opdycke's preparations fell apart. But then the commander of the 73rd Illinois, Maj. Thomas Motherspaw, shouted, "Go for them boys!" and it was like a dam breaking. Opdycke's regiments all gave a shout and surged forward up the slopes of the hill toward the breach and the Carter house. Opdycke's men gave extra punch now to the defense, which was holding its own. The push would forever seal the breach and Hood's opportunity for victory.

West of the turnpike, the 24th Wisconsin, led by 19-year-old Maj. Arthur MacArthur, shouted as it charged into the very yard of the Carter house. Some of the men rushed into the house itself to use it for cover. MacArthur led most of his men into the chaotic melee around the Carter house, where his horse was shot, spilling him to the ground. He arose, sword in hand. When he was wounded in the shoulder, he kept on, pushing his way toward a Confederate flag held by a major, who shot him in the chest. MacArthur staggered, yet stabbed the Confederate with his sword, killing him, but not before the Confederate officer shot the Union officer once more. MacArthur collapsed

Markers tell the story of the charge of Opdycke's men. (wlw)

with his dead foe. Fortunately, his men managed to get him to safety, and despite the three wounds, he eventually recovered, later to become father of Gen. Douglas MacArthur.

All around, similar deeds played out in a maddening sequence of brutality as the gray soldiers pushed on through the Carter house grounds and back to the main line of works. Another member of the 24th said they "went for the Johnnies, who had to retreat again to the other side of the rifle pits. We fired as fast as we could. . . ." A member of the 88th Illinois said they "used bayonets, buts of guns, axes, picks, and shovels. . . . Opdycke picked up a gun and clubbed with it. . . . Capt. Barnard . . . used a little old four-barrel pistol and even a hatchet that he always carried with him. . . ."

\*     \*     \*

East of the pike, Confederates were staggered by the surge of the 8th Tennessee, the 12th and 16th Kentucky, and the 175th Ohio as they were joined by Opdycke's forces. Brutality ruled the day. "It would be impossible to picture that scene in all its horrors," recalled Colonel Samuel Wolff. "I saw a Confederate soldier, close to me, thrust one of our men through with the bayonet, and before he could draw his weapon from the ghastly wound his brains were scattered on all of us that stood near, by the butt of a musket swung with terrific force by some big fellow. . . . And as I glanced hurriedly around and heard the dull thuds, I turned from the sickening sight."

Rushing forward with this part of the line was General Stanley, who had been in town resting at Schofield's headquarters. But with the sound of battle, he rode to the front while Schofield moved his headquarters to Fort Granger. Encountering Wagner's refugees and then riding among Opdycke's men, urging them onward, Stanley quickly entered the swirl of battle. He just as quickly went out, severely wounded—the highest-ranking Union casualty of the fight.

The breach was now sealed east of the turnpike, though the killing would continue on for some time in earnest, becoming what one Confederate called "a chamber of horrors." Indeed, the viciousness of the fight can be seen in the actions of Capt. A. P. Baldwin

As Opdycke smashed into the Carter House yard, across the turnpike, Unionist Tennesseans and Kentuckians, joined by newly enlisted Ohioans, pitched into Cleburne's veterans near the Lotz House and began to force them back, foot by bloody foot. (wlw)

of the 6th Ohio Artillery. He posted on the line at an angle near the cotton gin where he, in the words of Captain Schofield "took advantage of the situation, and to mow down the dense forest of humanity he loaded his guns to the muzzles with triple rounds of canister and dummies made with stockings which the gunners took from their feet, and filled with bullets from the infantry ammunition boxes." Baldwin noted, "At every discharge of my gun there were two distinct sounds: first explosion and then the bones."

\* \* \*

Brig. Gen. States Rights Gist seemed fated to fight for the Confederacy with such a name. Serving at First Manassas as an aide for the ill-fated General Bernard Bee, he now met the same fate as Bee in the darkness at Franklin. (loc)

The left end of Cheatham's division moved onward without Bate to their left. Leading the way forward beside Gordon was States Rights Gist. Gist was out front on his horse, hat in hand, encouraging his Georgians and South Carolinians forward, while General Carter moved in support. "We beheld the magnificent spectacle the battlefield presented, bands were playing, general and staff officers were riding in front of and between the lines, 100 battle-flags were waving in the smoke of battle, while 20,000 brave men were marching in perfect order against the foe," recalled Colonel Ellison Capers of the 24th South Carolina. He further described, "The sight inspired every man of the Twenty-fourth with the sentiment of duty. As we were pressing back the enemy's advance forces Lieut. Col. J. S. Jones fell mortally wounded in front of the right of the regiment, General Gist . . . rode down our front, and returning ordered the charge." With a shout and cheer, Gist's men rushed forward into the low ground fronting the Union line west of the

**Vicious hand-to-hand combat swirled around the Carter House and outbuildings.** (wlw)

Columbia Turnpike. Gist's route brought him over some of the rolling ground west of the pike and toward the looming thicket of the locust grove, whose jagged branches gave an eerie appearance.

"General Gist rode up to me in the course of the battle and called out excitedly . . . 'Colonel, I count on the 24th today,'" Capers said. "I kissed my hand to him, as he rode away. . . . " That was the last time Capers and the South Carolinians saw their general. Somewhere near the locust grove, a shot killed his horse, and as the general moved forward on foot, he was shot in the chest and killed.

Like Gordon's men beside them, Gist's men struck the works, some without official leadership: "Most of our commanding officers had been killed or wounded, and we did not know who was in command, when we took their breastworks our color bearer struck his flag staff in the top of the works and Company C, Ninety-seventh Ohio Regiment, tried to take the flag from him," one South Carolinian recalled. "After firing two or three rounds, they lay down in the ditches, and we would get the guns of the wounded men, put the bayonets on them and pitch them point foremost on them, Then we pushed the logs from the top of the works, which were from ten to twelve inches thick, on to them. They remained in the ditch until we started to charge the second time, and when we jumped into the ditches we took them prisoner," said the Southern soldier about his comrades' efforts.

But no progress could be made. Even as the Tennesseans of Carter's brigade came up, with

**General John C. Carter, promoted the previous July around Atlanta, became another casualty for Hood's army. He was carried back to the Harrison house, where he died on December 10th, 1864.** (cmh)

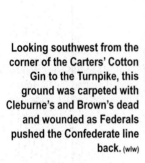

Looking southwest from the corner of the Carters' Cotton Gin to the Turnpike, this ground was carpeted with Cleburne's and Brown's dead and wounded as Federals pushed the Confederate line back. (wlw)

their commander mortally wounded, they just piled more men into the ditch and added to the surreal scene that now played out.

Nearby, Gordon found the position his men occupied untenable, subjected to a brutal enfilade fire—the line east of the pike ran at an angle to their position in the ditch in front of the Carter garden. Gordon later wrote:

> *the fatality to us, as we crouched and fought in the ditch, became so great from these three fires—front, left and rear—that some of the men shouted to the enemy across the line that if they would 'cease firing' they would surrender. Amid the uproar this was not heard, and a signal of surrender was made by putting our hats or caps on their bayonets fixed on their guns and holding them up above the works. The first of these signals that were seen were perforated by the enemy's bullets. I suppose they thought it was our heads, or they did not know what it meant. At length, however, they heard and understood our men, and amid the fearful din, we distinctly heard the command, 'Cease firing!' given on the other side of the works; and in a moment more all was comparatively quiet in our immediate front, and the men walked over the works and surrendered. It was fatal to leave the ditch and attempt to escape to the rear. Every man who attempted it—and a number did—was at once shot down. I ordered them to remain in the ditch until I told them they could surrender. When all had walked over the works except one of*

*my men and myself he asked if I was not going over. I replied in the negative, saying that I would remain under cover of the dead in the ditch until night, which was approaching. He said he would remain with me. But the bullets from our rear and the enfilading fire on our left (and which had never ceased) fell so thickly about us that, I finally said 'We shall be killed if we remain here,' at the same time handing him a white handkerchief and telling him to put it on his bayonet and walk over the works. He did so and I followed him.*

**Pock marks from bullets scar the brick wall of one of the Carter house outbuildings. (cm)**

For others, the fighting continued along the line as darkness settled over the field like a heavy shroud and the roar of battle sounded once again to the left.

Bate was finally going in.

# *Upon Us like Tigers*
## *Bate's Attack*

## CHAPTER TWELVE
*November 30, 1864–5:00 p.m.*

As the rest of Cheatham's Corps slammed into the Union defenses, the men that composed Gen. "Billy" Bate's division of 2,100 Tennesseans, Georgians, and Floridians rushed to catch up. They had to make their way through a gap in the range of hills and then arc up near the Carter Creek Pike—a detour that delayed them considerably.

Bate advanced in a similar fashion to the rest of the corps with two of his three brigades on line: Brig. Gen. Thomas Benton Smith's Tennesseans and Georgians; Brig. Gen. Henry Rootes Jackson's Georgians; and one in reserve, Col. Robert Bullock's Floridians. They moved through the fields around the widow Rebecca Bostick plantation, "Everbright"—a two-story brick Greek revival-style mansion with a columned front, built on a slight rise. Around Everbright, Bate's men began to come under fire from Union skirmishers who fell back toward their main line, but Bate's brigades swept steadily onward.

But a problem soon became apparent. Just as his delay had left Brown's left flank in the air, now Bate found that Chalmer's cavalrymen were nowhere to be seen on his own left. To deal with this unexpected danger, Bate sent orders to Col. Robert Bullock to move his brigade of Floridians from their position in reserve and take position on the division left, astride the Carter Creek Pike. Bate now rolled forward in a single line of battle with no reserves.

Two-hundred thirty Tennesseans, many of whom fell in the repulse of Brown's and Bate's Divisions, lie buried in the Carnton Confederate Cemetery today. (cm)

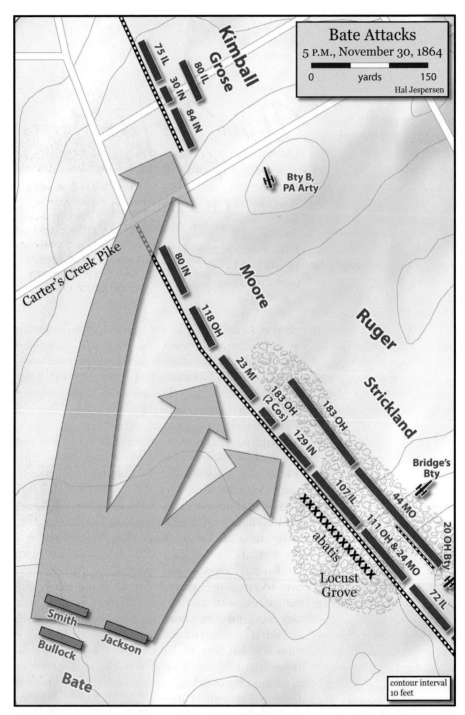

**BATE ATTACKS**—Having to swing around the Confederate left to move into the fight, Bate's division struck west of the Carter House farm in the growing darkness. Like all the other attacks, it met with a bloody repulse after some of the war's most intense fighting.

The ground over which they advanced was a rolling series of swales similar to the terrain east of the turnpike. Indeed, the ground and decreasing light had deceived Bate that Chalmer's troopers were actually on his left but invisible to him.

Bate's brigades now unknowingly advanced past their flank protection toward the waiting soldiers of Ruger's and Kimball's divisions. "The assault on the works was made . . . with courage and vigor rarely equaled in ancient or modern warfare," Bate attested. His right brigade, General Jackson's Georgians, found the tangled and swampy Locust Grove looming on his right and center just as the dreaded popping of exploding shells began to rain shrapnel down upon them. Lyman Bridge's Illini and Capt. Jacob Zeigler's Pennsylvania Battery worked their cannon, hurling shell and case shot over the Union line and into the rushing gray line in a murderous crossfire. As the Confederates neared the Union line, they gained a momentary respite as they swept down into a final swale before emerging about 150 yards from the Union earthworks and into seemingly unending volleys of musketry and artillery fire. General Ruger noted that the line began to "gradually waste and disappear." But some struggled onward, and raising the rebel yell, they pitched toward their tormentors.

Jackson's Georgians and Smith's Tennesseans headed toward Col. Orlando Moore's brigade's defenses. In Smith's brigade, one of his regiments, the 20th Tennessee, moved forward with stronger vigor. Many of its men hailed from Middle Tennessee, and quite a few called Franklin, and Williamson County, home. Notable among them was one of Smith's staff officers, Capt. Theodrick "Tod" Carter, who now saw his father's farm rising to his right. Just before the assault, he had asked—and received permission from—Smith to go into the attack with his old command. As the Tennesseans neared the line, Tod urged his comrades onward and then spurred his horse toward home. He only made it a short distance when he and his horse were struck with a hail of bullets. Tod was thrown forward and sprawled on the ground, grievously wounded with five injuries, a little more than 500 feet away from his home.

The rest of Smith's men continued on, as did Jackson's Georgians, though their lines were being thinned at every step. The remains of the

General William Bate was a hard-fighting commander, known for his bravery on the battlefield, but he was not well liked by some of his men, who thought he would see them in their graves if it meant a promotion for him. (loc)

The 183rd Ohio, along with the 44th Missouri and 175th Ohio, were all recently raised regiments. Instrumental in stopping the Confederate breakthroughs, they defied stereotypes of green troops wavering under fire. (wlw)

Youthful General Thomas Benton Smith led his brigade forward into action near the Locust Thicket. (cmh)

Colonel Mervin Clark was a well-liked and respected officer despite his youth. Having served in both the Eastern and Western Theaters as a member of the 7th Ohio Infantry, he became the colonel of the 183rd in the fall of 1864. (oiw)

locust grove—and the abatis that many of its trees had become—tore and slashed at the men as they struggled through the morass, but they managed to make it to Moore's works. "The Rebels came upon us like tigers," one soldier recalled.

Then, an opportunity for the gray soldiers presented itself. Two companies of new recruits from the 183rd Ohio held a portion of the line to their front, but the fury of the attack was more than they could stand. The Buckeyes broke, opening a gap. Not far to the rear was the balance of the 183rd in the second line of works, already taking losses because Bate's men were firing high. Lieutenant Colonel Mervin Clark, just 21 years old, ordered his men forward to the main line. Grabbing the regimental colors, he led the way, where he mounted the works for a few moments, urging his men on—but then he fell dead, shot at his moment of triumph.

Clark's men, though, bought time, and while they could not retake the position, they gave Moore the opportunity to bring in reinforcements and drive the Confederates back. As they regained the works, one Michigander remembered hearing almost visceral agony: "Oh! Such groaning and praying and pleading I never heard before, and God knows that I do not want to again."

Bate attempted more attacks, and although some of the fighting was hand to hand, his men achieved no further breaks. "The Federal line . . . looked the more grim and angry as the smoke of battle thickened and the shadows of the evening darker grew," Bate observed. "The approaching night also gave increased glare to the sheets of flame as they

Looking toward the location of the Locust Grove from Carter House Hill. (wlw)

leaped from beneath the 'headlogs' on the crest of the earthworks, as shot and shell and minie balls were launched upon the advancing lines." Smith and Jackson's men either huddled in the trenches or fell back to one of the nearby swales for cover.

* * *

As the Georgians and Tennesseans made their charge, Bullock's Floridians advanced farther to the west. In their front, Kimball's division's line angled back to the northwest to touch the Harpeth. As their comrades came under fire to the east of the Carter's Creek Pike, Bullock's men were still making their way toward the Union line. Having to cross the entire brigade to the western side of the pike, they passed a little schoolhouse where they became engaged with Col. Thomas Rose's 77th Pennsylvania, posted as skirmishers along Kimball's front. The Pennsylvanians put up strong resistance—no doubt inspired by a desire not to be captured again as many of them had at the battle of Chickamauga the year before. They held out longer than a skirmish line should, and only when his left was being turned did Rose order his men back toward the main line, clearing the front so that at about 250 yards, Kimball's line opened fire on the Floridians. "Our boys began dropping like corn before a hail storm," Henry Reddick of the 1st Florida remembered.

The left wing of the determined advance moved into a narrow ravine of a tributary of the Harpeth, where destruction seemed to rain down on them. Lieutenant Colonel Edward Badger tried to push his men forward, but he soon fell with three wounds. The command to lie down soon passed down the line, and the men hugged the ground, and for about 10 minutes they endured. But then many of them cracked and began to fly back to the rear in confusion, and more blasts of fire sped them along into the darkness.

Some remained, Reddick among them. "It was the only hope," he admitted, "for we could neither go forward or go back in such a fire and live. . . . We laid there under that terrific fire until about eleven when all at once the firing ceased."

Captain Tod Carter fell in battle on his family farm, died of his wounds in his own bed, and was then buried near his family. (wlw)

# Moving into the Very Door of Hell
## Johnson's Night Attack

### CHAPTER THIRTEEN
*November 30, 1864–7:00 p.m.*

As Cheatham's and Stewart's men grappled with Cox's and Stanley's men, S. D. Lee's corps and the army's artillery began to arrive, marching through the twilight on the Columbia Turnpike. The sound of thousands of marching feet and the cracking of gravel under the hooves and rolling wheels of the artillery joined the sounds of battle echoing off the surrounding hills as the corps made its way into the gap between Breezy and Winstead hills.

Lee reported to Hood at the Neeley house to ask for orders and was told to take his first two divisions, Johnson's and Clayton's, and position them to support the attack and then to report to Cheatham. Lee rode the short distance in the growing darkness to Cheatham's headquarters at Privet Knob. "I met General Cheatham about dark," he recalled, "and was informed by him that assistance was needed at once." Lee asked where he was needed, and Cheatham pointed to the front, saying, "Yonder line of fire at the breastworks is where you are needed and wanted at once." Lee ordered Edward Johnson to move immediately.

"Old Alleghany" Johnson began to deploy his four brigades as twilight turned into night, moving toward the Confederate left. As Johnson made his way in the growing darkness, Cheatham and Bate both met him and warned him of the presence of their own men at the front and cautioned him not to fire into them. Arriving behind Everbright Mansion,

The Carter House, visible in the distance from the ground where Johnson's men attacked, faded from view as darkness settled over the battlefield. (cm)

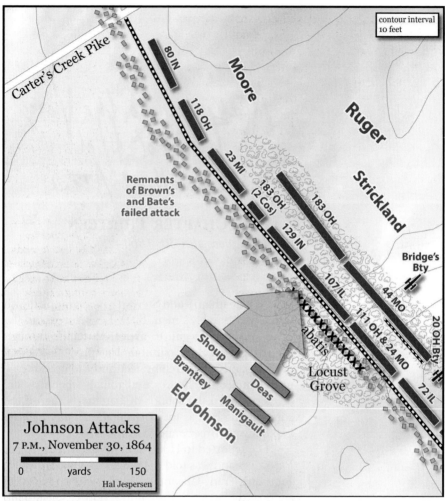

**Johnson Attacks**
7 P.M., November 30, 1864

0    yards    150
Hal Jespersen

**JOHNSON ATTACKS—Night attacks were a relatively rare occurrence on a Civil War battlefield, and the assault of General Ed Johnson's division serves to illustrate why. His men stumbled through the darkness and over obstacles, including fallen soldiers from earlier attacks. Confusion and chaos reigned, and the attack sputtered to a halt before striking the blazing Union earthworks the men were guiding on.**

Johnson prepared to advance in support of Bate's left. Men lit torches and gave them to the right and left guides of each regiment, and soon orders to advance were given.

Johnson moved forward with Brig. Gen. Jacob Sharp's Mississippi Brigade on the front left; Brig. Gen. Zachariah Deas's Alabama Brigade on the front right; Brigadier General Brantley's Mississippians on the rear left in support of Sharp; and Brig. Gen. Arthur Manigault's South Carolinians and Alabamians in support of Deas. It was now about 7 p.m., completely dark, and the temperature was growing colder. "The noble veterans of Johnson's division heeded not all these discouraging features," General Lee noted, "but intent on carrying succor and a fresh supply of ammunition to their struggling comrades in front. . . ."

Johnson's division moved forward quietly toward the Union entrenchments. "The shadows of coming night had settled heavily around us just as we came in range of their rifles and nerved ourselves for the charge," a member of the 41st Mississippi recalled. "We were ordered to omit the usual yell, conceal our approach under cover of the darkness, and make a spirited dash for the works." The front line had been bolstered by the advance of Brantley's brigade of Mississippians, who were ordered to move to extend the front as they rushed toward the Union line.

A Federal soldier, straining his eyes into the darkness to see their advance, later testified, "It was very near dark when they made their second charge. They came two and three lines deep, and as they reached the top of the ridge they raised the rebel yell and rushed right up to the outer edge of our works, and some were killed on top of the works."

Observing the fight, General Lee later said, "It looked as if the division was moving into the very door of hell, lighted up with its sulphurous flames." One of Johnson's men, in the thick of that fight, said the line was "belching flash and flame of lurid fire, and smoking like the crater of a volcano. . . ."

Sharp and a portion of Deas's men went crashing through the thorny thicket of the remains of the now-splintered locust grove, hitting the works with full force and driving back a portion of the Union line, capturing three stands of colors. "You cannot have the slightest imagination of how many men were killed . . ." one of Deas's Alabamians wrote. "Such a slaughter of men never was seen before. . . ."

A savage hand-to-hand fight ensued. At points, combatants could only see their foes by the flashing of the musket and cannon blasts. "They charged us . . . and fought with the most determination I ever saw," marveled Corporal J. A. Morlan of the 107th Illinois. "There were seven or eight stands of colors planted on our regt's works, and the top of the works lined thick with Rebs three or four times. But we shot, bayoneted, and knocked them off with the butts of our guns. . . ." In this hellacious struggle, Sharp was wounded, along with most of the regimental commanders of his brigade, with one killed on top of the works, leaving only company-grade officers.

Confederates now had a slight lodgment, but the

1864 was a trying year for Marylander Edward Johnson. Captured in the brutal fighting at Spotsylvania in the spring, he was exchanged by late summer and sent to the Army of Tennessee to replace the foppish Thomas Hindman in command of one of the army's best divisions. (loc)

General Zachariah Cantey Deas hailed from a prominent South Carolina family, but was trying his fortunes in Mobile, Alabama, when the war broke out, so he went to war at the head of Alabama troops. (loc)

General Arthur Middleton Manigault was a veteran of the Mexican War, fighting with South Carolina's famed Palmetto Regiment. A rice planter in the South Carolina lowlands, he raised and commanded the 10th South Carolina in the early days of the war. His leadership was rewarded with promotion to brigade command. (loc)

darkness and chaos made it impossible to capitalize upon it. They did fire into the flanks of nearby Union troops, but made no real progress beyond the initial breakthrough. Years afterward, a member of the 24th Mississippi surmised that "It was the crowning wave of Southern valor, endurance and vengeance . . . that dashed its crest into bloody foam on the breastworks. . . ."

\*    \*    \*

To the left of Deas and Sharp, farther to the west near the Carter Creek Pike, Brantley's men struggled forward toward the line. But as they rushed forward, their front suddenly opened with blasts of fire. Incoming fire came, too, from the defenses on the west side of the Carter Creek Pike. The crossfire shredded the Mississippians' line. "When about forty steps from the works we received a volley of musketry that made a considerable thinning in our lines," reported Robert A. Jarman of the 27th Mississippi, "but we raised a shout and went at them with loaded guns and carried the works by storm. . . ."

"This was where the bayonet and gunstock was used to effect," recalled R. H. Cocke of the 24th Mississippi. "It was here, more than anywhere else, that I least expected to ever see my mother again."

But Brantley's men were unable to breach the position and were forced to hunker down in the ditch in front of the works. As a testament to the carnage, one Mississippian noted, "The blood actually ran in the ditch . . . and in places saturated our clothing, where we were lying down."

Johnson ordered Manigault to move his brigade up from its position in reserve to help Brantley, directing the brigade toward the Carter's Creek Pike to extend the line in that direction—what one officer called "a share of the bloody work." The move proved to be quite difficult in the murky darkness and while under fire. Lieutenant Colonel C. Irvine Walker, commanding the 10th South Carolina, wrote:

*As we were advancing under fire, across an open field, my Regiment was marching with military precision and in such splendid line that I was proud of my men. I jumped into the line and looking to my right and to my left, found the line as perfect as on dress*

*parade. But we struck a deep ditch and I called out "can you jump it?" I was answered "Oh yes, Colonel." But I thought best to halt the Regiment and see for myself. It was so dark I could see nothing, so I made one man try to jump it and he was lost head over heels. Just then a Staff Officer rode up and advised me that Genl. Manigault had been wounded. The ditch was made by a stream from a spring house. I moved the Regiment around its head and formed on the enemy's side. The delay of this movement caused me to lose our touch to the left, which we were ordered to observe, our Regiment being on the right of the Brigade. I then moved to our left to find the Brigade to secure my position. I found them across a pike among some hills in considerable confusion, with Col. Shaw riding furiously about, shouting, "forward, men, forward!" I went to him and suggested that before moving forward he had best get the Brigade in order, to which he assented, forming on my Regiment. We were then covered by a slight depression in the ground. When formed we were moved forward and hardly uncovered ourselves before Col. Shaw was wounded and Col. Davis of the 24th Ala. took command, but he was wounded about two minutes later. There we were, without orders, lost on the battlefield at night. I did not like the situation. . . .*

Alone on the field, Walker did the most sensible

The flash of the guns illuminated Johnson's attack in the darkness—a hellish experience for all concerned. (nps)

Lt. Col. C. Irvine Walker, a Citadel graduate in the Class of 1861, served most of the war on Manigault's staff before being promoted to command the 10th South Carolina in the fighting around Atlanta. He was severely wounded in the neck at Ezra Church, but returned in time to lead his regiment in the Tennessee Campaign. (nps)

**View of Carter House Hill from the ground over which Johnson's night assault stumbled forward.** (wlw)

thing: He ordered his men to halt and lie down while he sent a courier to General Johnson to advise him of the situation. Walker later wrote in the history of the 10th South Carolina: "[A]n officer was sent to find out what orders we were acting under—the men being needlessly slaughtered. Three successive brigade commanders and the only staff officer who knew anything of the movement had been wounded and carried from the field. Genl Edward Johnson being found, approved our action, and knowing that the entire attack had failed, withdrew us a short distance. . . ."

Johnson's attack "was foredoomed to failure. Johnson's men served but to increase the heaps of dead and wounded which strewed the field," stated one soldier in the 111th Ohio. The attack ended the Confederate offensives. But along the lines where only a matter of feet separated the combatants, the battle for life or death continued.

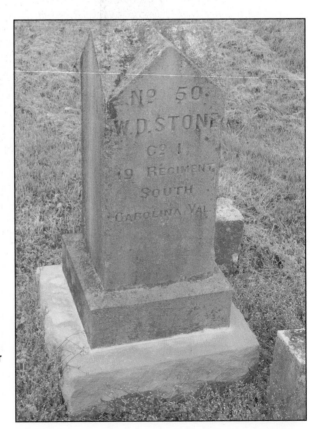

**Sgt. William D. Stone, a middle-class farmer from near Abbeville, South Carolina, fell in the attack made by Ed Johnson's Division on the night of November 30.** (wlw)

Bullet holes pock the wooden
walls of one of the Carter
house outbuildings—
a testament to the ferocity of
the fighting. (cm)

# All Along the Line

## CHAPTER FOURTEEN

### November 30–December 1, 1864

Though the battle of Franklin is said to have lasted five hours, the majority of the fighting occurred over a period of only about two hours—those being some of the bloodiest and most intense minutes of the entire war. But with Ed Johnson's final attack, the fighting settled into a more savage and personal nature.

The men in gray tried to keep up the fight—either from positions they had withdrawn to a short distance away from the works, where they had tried to take cover, or along the line of entrenchments where they still huddled in the trenches. Others simply tried to stay alive, while still others, reaching the breaking point of endurance and seeing no other option, did as Gordon had and surrendered.

Some of the men stayed longer than others, joined by more men from other commands with each successive attack. In front of the cotton gin, survivors of the Missouri brigade were joined by men from Sears's and Adams's brigades; men from Cleburne's and even Brown's divisions crammed together in the ditch, while others found shelter in the swales and gullies over which they had come to reach the fight.

The repulse of Johnson, however, convinced Hood not to try any more assaults that evening. "The two remaining divisions, Major Generals Henry D. Clayton's and Carter Stevenson's, could not unfortunately become engaged owing to the

**Many of the Confederate dead still lay on the field.** (cm)

**Blasts of canister added flashes of hell to the fight that continued on into the darkness.** (bal)

obscurity of night," he later wrote. Instead, he initially wanted the two remaining divisions to be ready to attack in the morning after a bombardment of the Union positions by the artillery, which was now all on the field—though he learned from both Cheatham and Stewart that they seriously doubted their commands would be of any use due to their decimated and disorganized condition.

West of the Columbia Turnpike, General Strahl was in the trenches with his men and aiding them in their fight across the trenches. As with other officers, the fighting had created a situation where one's rank did not account for much, and officers fought as their men did. Sergeant Sumner Cunningham of the 41st Tennessee recounted Strahl's final exploits:

> *[W]e fired at the flash of each other's guns. . . . Holding the enemy's lines, as we continued to do on this part of them, we were terribly massacred by the enfilade firing. The works were so high that those who fired the guns were obliged to get a footing in the embankment, exposing themselves in addition to their flank, to fire by men in houses. One especially severe was from Mr. Carter's, immediately in my front. I was near Gen. Strahl, who stood in the ditch, and handed up guns to those posted to fire them. The man who had been firing cocked it and was taking deliberate*

*aim, when he was shot and tumbled down dead into the ditch upon those killed before him. When the men so exposed were shot down, their places were supplied by volunteers until these were exhausted, and it was necessary for Gen. Strahl to call upon others. He turned to me, and though I was several feet back from the ditch, I rose up immediately, and walking over the wounded and dead, took position with one foot upon the piled of bodies of my dead fellows, and the other in the embankment, and fired guns which the General himself handed up to me until he too was shot down. One other man had position on my right, and assisted in the firing.*

*The battle lasted until not an efficient man was left between us and the Columbia Pike, about fifty yards to our right, and hardly enough behind us to hand up the guns. We could not hold out much longer, for indeed, but few of us were then left alive. It seemed as if we had no choice but to surrender or try to get away, and when I asked the General for counsel, he simply answered, 'Keep firing.'*

*A grim sense of resolution set in then [among the] men along the lines, though many of them knew that if the fighting kept up, many of them would not make it til dawn. Indeed, a few minutes after Cunningham spoke, General Strahl was wounded again, and then while being carried to the rear was struck a third time and killed.*

In Cleburne's front, his men began to wonder

**The damage still visible upon the buildings of the Carter Farm are a testimony to the intensity of the fighting that swirled around them on the evening of November 30, 1864. They remain some of the most battle-scarred structures in all of North America.** (wlw)

**Brutal hand-to-hand fighting erupted periodically in the darkness.** (tya)

A graduate of Nashville's Western Military Institute in 1859, Gordon rose to the rank of general despite his youth. Gordon was 28 when he received his promotion in August of 1864. (loc)

General Otho F. Strahl was born in Ohio, but died fighting for the Confederacy in Tennessee. (bat)

where he was and what he would have them do. "You see, we kept getting over, but they would reinforce and drive us out," one of Cleburne's veterans explained. "And finally we said, 'let's pass the word along the line to keep quiet till General Cleburne gives the word to charge. . . . We waited and waited and waited. And the boys kept crying for the word and wondered why it didn't come. But when it didn't come, I knew Pat Cleburne was dead; for if he had been living he would have given us that order."

Brown's men also heard nothing. Brown had been wounded in the attack and all of his brigade commanders were down, as well—killed or wounded—as were many regimental commanders, like Colonel Capers, so no one knew who held command of the division or, for that matter, even of some brigades. In the ditch near the shattered locust grove there was still fight in the men of Gist's brigade—Lt. James Tillman of the 24th South Carolina being one. "Jim Tillman never wanted inspiration to duty," Capers remembered. "He led the men over, and that night gave me the flag of the 97th Ohio. . . ." They were not able to make anything more of it, though. Sporadic flare ups and small-scale sorties like Tillman's continued until after 9 p.m., when finally it all started to die down and a new nightmare began.

\*      \*      \*

As the sun set and the final attacks slammed into the Union entrenchments, the temperature steadily ticked downward, and now the men began

The line of gravel marks the Union line east of the Turnpike. (wlw)

In the aftermath of the battle, Carnton became a field hospital. Bloodstains are still visible throughout the house *(wlw)*

to feel the bite of December cold as the final hours of November slipped away. For the wounded, the dropping temperature added yet another level of agony for them—and without the roar of gunfire, the cries of the wounded became more noticeable. "Nothing could be heard but the wails of the wounded and the dying," a surviving officer in the 1st Missouri recalled with a chill, "some calling for their friends, some praying to be relieved of their awful suffering, and thousands in the deep, agonizing throes of death filled the air with mournful sounds and dying groans."

Adjutant Robert W. Banks of the 29th Alabama wrote, "the groans and frenzied cries of the wounded on both sides of the earthworks were awe inspiring. The ravings of the maimed and mangled . . .were heart rending. . . ." The agony only grew worse as the temperature continued to fall and the wind, blowing in from the north, began to be keenly felt.

\*     \*     \*

As the firing finally sputtered out, Schofield made his way back from Fort Granger—where he had stayed through most of the battle—and into the town. The bridge repairs had wrapped up, and all of his wagons had made their way across the Harpeth, so he now issued orders for his men to withdraw from their positions at midnight and make their way on to Nashville.

**Some of the most traumatic moments of the battle occurred in the fighting that took place after the main attacks had stopped.** (wlw)

The idea of withdrawing from the field of horror was fine with some men, but others were shocked and upset to leave the hard-fought field on which they had just devastated Hood's army. "A lieutenant standing near me said, 'We ought to remain here and wipe hell out of 'em,' when I promptly replied, 'There is no hell left in them. Don't you hear them praying?'" recalled brigade commander Col. Israel Stiles. "I was warranted in making this statement, for at the time I heard more appealing prayers from those poor suffering Confederates on the other side of the hedge than I ever heard before or since. . . ."

Jacob Cox also wanted to hold on and finish Hood's army. However, Schofield was satisfied with being able to get out with his army intact. Indeed, he had lost around 2,500 men in the conflict—most of whom were from Wagner's two exposed brigades in the advance line—with probably 350 to 400 of that number killed. Still unnerved and on edge from the series of close calls he'd had, and despite the protests, Schofield ordered his men off the field. By 3 a.m., the last of the exhausted Union forces were out of their works and moving through Franklin and on to Nashville, leaving the field to the Confederates.

Although the Confederates did not realize for some time that their foes were gone, they did take the opportunity of the subsided firing to begin moving their wounded from the field. The search for the survivors began, too, as men wandered looking for friends. One such man combing the battlefield was Lycurgus Sallee, one of the hand-picked men that made up the Army of Tennessee's Whitworth

sharpshooter corps. "The most destructive fire, as the general charge was made, came from just east of the pike and was directed against the left of Govan's Arkansas brigade, notably the Sixth Arkansas Regiment, and was made by perhaps less than a regiment of Yankees . . ." he said.

This illustration shows the damage to the Carter Farm in the aftermath of the battle. The buildings witnessed some of the most severe fighting of the entire war. (bal)

> *It appeared as if almost every shot had taken effect. Such execution was very rare at the first volley from the men behind earthworks. . . . Here among the dead and wounded I found many friends and acquaintances, including the sergeants and two members of our sharpshooters. . . . I followed the line of works west of the pike, where Cheatham's division charged, and all indications showed that the struggle had been of the same desperate character . . . the dead being strewn all along the line. I also noticed here a grove of black locust trees six to eight inches in diameter many of which was shot down with Minie balls.*

Eventually Confederates discovered that Schofield had escaped and that the Army of Tennessee held the field, technically giving them a victory by default—but few of those who had survived felt like it.

Today, most of the Confederate dead from the battle rest in the McGavock Confederate Cemetery at Carnton, buried in state sections. (wlw)

# The Cost of Victory

## CONCLUSION
### December 1864

As the pink dawn brought light to the frigid landscape, daylight illuminated a horrific scene. The ground for several yards in front of the entrenchments was a carpet of frost-covered bodies. The heart and soul of the Army of Tennessee lay there on the ground, on the white gravel of the Columbia Turnpike, draped upon the thick Osage orange hedge, in the yard of the Carter house, laying over the headlogs and piled in the ditches of the now-abandoned Union earthworks. Light gave proof to the tragic landscape and confirmation of the worst fears of the men.

"Early on the following morning after the battle," recollected William "Goose" Gibson of the 6th Arkansas,

> *Wm. Minton, a member of my company, and myself started out to hunt for our dead as well as such of our wounded comrades had been unable to leave the field. We soon became separated, however . . . . I looked around for Minton, and failing to see him, procured other help and carried the man back to our field hospital, which was located something like a mile south of the battleground.*
>
> *Returning to the field, I met Minton with another one*

Most of the Confederates killed in the battle were initially buried in the ditch in front of the Union earthworks. Later, they were removed by the efforts of Carrie McGavock and buried upon her Carnton Plantation. (cm)

*of our wounded boys, who, upon my inquiry as to his identity, told me that just after our separation he and some others, who like ourselves were looking for their comrades, had found Gen. Cleburne's body. . . . To my further inquiries, he told me the general, when found, was lying on his face just inside the enemy's works, shot through the body, his pockets were turned wrong side out, and his boots and sword and belt were gone. Soon, after this, Minton pointed out to me the precise spot on which the general's body lay when found. This, as I have said was just inside the works, and as I now remember it, some twenty five or thirty feet east of a line drawn due south from the southeast corner of the old gin house. . . . It was the accepted opinion of everyone there at the time, that he was killed on top of the works and had either fallen or been pulled over inside. Whilst standing at this point I well remember being shown the position of his head and feet when found and the pool of blood which in its flow, carried with it the life of our beloved, our brave and matchless general.*

Another who saw Cleburne's body that morning, John McQuade, remembered, "He lay flat upon his back as if asleep, his military cap partly over his eyes. He had on a new gray uniform, the coat of the sack or blouse pattern. It was unbuttoned and open; the lower part of his vest was unbuttoned and open. He wore a white linen shirt, which was stained with blood on the front part of the left side, or just left of the abdomen. This was the only sign of a wound I saw on him, and I believe it is the only one he had received."

Cleburne was one of the six Confederate generals dead or dying, besides seven wounded, and one missing—now a prisoner of war. The officer corps of the Confederate army, for all purposes, was gone: Already critically damaged in the struggle for Atlanta, it all but ceased to exist now. Indeed, a Union soldier said that the conduct of the officers was something he had never seen before: "The Rebs fought desperately. Colonels and Generals rode right up to our faces bringing their men up in fine style but 'blue coats' wouldn't budge back one inch and they fell victims of their own mad actions."

The loss of officers in some commands seemed to leave the Southern soldiers at a loss for what to do now, Mississippian R. H. Cocke admitted. "The next morning when we attempted to reorganize my regiment, there were only forty-four to be found," he said, "and among them not a commissioned officer, all either being dead or wounded, and for seventy five yards on either side of the works we could have walked upon the dead without ever stepping on the ground."

Most damaging of all to Hood's forces was the loss of soldiers. Although General Hood would report to Richmond that his losses were "about 4,500," there is some evidence that it was much higher, maybe even as high as 7,500, of which at least 1,750 were dead. Some of the best and storied units of the army were gutted and would never perform the same way on the field of battle again.

The magnitude of death at Franklin often obscures the depth of personal tragedy that resulted from those deaths— one reason why the story of Tod Carter resonates so strongly. (cm)

Men gawked at what seemed to be acres of carnage. "The ditches on either side of the yankee works were literally filled with the dead and wounded—Yankees on the inside, and confederates on the outside," lamented Wesley Olin Connor of Georgia's Cherokee Light Artillery. "In some places would be found Yankees and Confederates piled upon each other. The main fighting was carried on across the works. In the road were eleven Yankees. In the yard of Mr. Carter were a large number of yankee dead. Around the well, where they had gone to get water they were lying thick, and the ground all around stained with blood. . . . I had long desired to visit a battlefield, but my curiosity is now fully satisfied."

Byron Bowers of Captain Beauregard's South Carolina Battery testified:

*Now I will say that in all of my over three years passed experience in the Civil War, I never had seen Confederate carnage so thick as it lay at Franklin, Tenn. Standing at the gap in the breastworks, where the turnpike road passed through, I think there must*

*have been two thousand dead Confederates in sight.
No picture could be made to portray the horrible scenes
presented by the undisturbed tenants left in possession
by the bloody fray the night before. The dead, cold
and stiff bodies were lying in every conceivable
posture, all with ghastly faces and glassy eyes. Some
lay with faces up and some with faces down, some in
a sitting attitude, braced with the dead bodies of their
comrades; some lay with two or three bodies on them.
Sometimes you could see a company commander
lying with sword in one hand and hat in the other.
Sometimes you could see a man who retained on his
face a martial frown; then again you see others who
wore a pleasing smile.*

\* \* \*

General Hood rode up the turnpike to see the
scene. "I rode over the scene of action . . . and could
but indulge in sad and painful thoughts as I beheld
so many brave soldiers struck down by the enemy
whom a few hours previous, at Spring Hill, we had
held within the palm of our hands," he later noted
with bitterness.

Many have labeled Hood a butcher and claim he
ordered the attack at Franklin to punish his army and
his men, but that notion is false. Hood mourned, evident
not only in his own words, but from the testimony of
witnesses as well. "General Hood stopped close to
where I was standing and took a long, retrospective
view of the arena of the awful contest. . . ." one soldier
reported. "His sturdy visage assumed a melancholy
appearance and for a considerable time he sat on his
horse and wept like a child."

The deaths of his soldiers struck Hood
profoundly, but he was also haunted by the idea that
had his orders been followed at Spring Hill, not only
would the disaster at Franklin have been averted,
but victory might well be theirs. Now, only a grave
awaited them, instead of a free home.

What to do now? Schofield had slipped away,
and Hood had no way of stopping him before he
arrived in Nashville. There, Thomas was receiving
other reinforcements, too: Major General Andrew
Jackson Smith's demi-corps of the Army of the
Tennessee, fresh off of their victory over Sterling
Price in Missouri.

Hood nonetheless sent orders for S. D. Lee to continue in pursuit with his corps, and for Bate to take his division and move eastward to invest and capture the Union garrison at Murfreesboro. There would be no rest for the weary. The remains of Cheatham's and Stewart's men took on the grim duty of burying their dead and taking stock of what remained.

When all that could be done was completed, the shadow of what was the heart and soul of the Army of Tennessee moved northward to the outskirts of Nashville, toward the "the darkest of all Decembers."

*    *    *

The armies' departure did not mean life returned to normal in Franklin. Every house became a hospital or held recovering men. Carnton, the MacGavock's mansion, saw the horrors of field surgery from the night of November 30 through the following days as surgeons dealt with the seemingly endless wounded from all across the Confederacy. Strangers from dirt farms in Mississippi died amid luxury they could have only dreamed of. At the Carter house, meanwhile, a more intimate case unfolded in the battle-damaged home: Tod Carter spent his last moments in the care of his family, dying in his own bed.

The recovery went on in town for the following weeks when the shambles of the Army of Tennessee returned, pursued by General Thomas's forces. The army could not linger, making its way rapidly southward. A few days earlier, on December 15 and 16, on the outskirts of Nashville, the inevitable had occurred: Thomas struck Hood's forces like a sledgehammer, shattering the already mortally wounded Southern army. During the pursuit, Franklin found Union soldiers occupying the town, taking prisoners of the Confederate wounded who were unable to move.

After this, the war left Franklin—in theory—but it left an indelible mark. The town remained haunted by the events of those hours of November 30, 1864, and the distant echoes can still be seen and felt today.

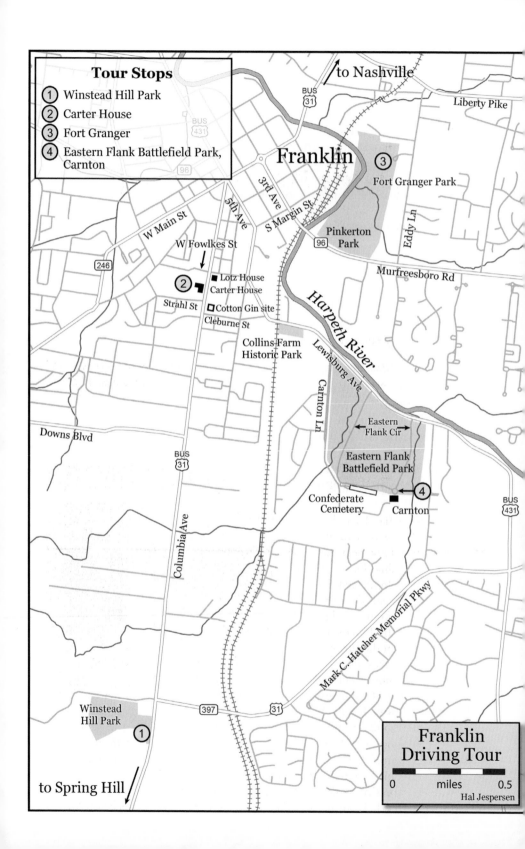

**Tour Stops**

1. Winstead Hill Park
2. Carter House
3. Fort Granger
4. Eastern Flank Battlefield Park, Carnton

to Nashville

Liberty Pike

BUS 31

BUS 431

96

Franklin

③ Fort Granger Park

3rd Ave

5th Ave

S Margin St

Eddy Ln

W Main St

Pinkerton Park

96

W Fowlkes St

Murfreesboro Rd

246

■ Lotz House

② Carter House

Strahl St   □ Cotton Gin site

Cleburne St

Collins Farm Historic Park

*Harpeth River*

Lewisburg Ave

Carnton Ln

Eastern Flank Cir

Downs Blvd

Eastern Flank Battlefield Park

BUS 31

Confederate Cemetery

Carnton

④

BUS 431

Columbia Ave

Mark C. Hatcher Memorial Pkwy

Winstead Hill Park

①

397   31

**Franklin Driving Tour**

0   miles   0.5

Hal Jespersen

to Spring Hill

# Touring the Battlefield

━━━━━━▶ **TO STOP 1**

*From I-75, take Exit 283 near Cartersville, Georgia. Travel east toward Allatoona Lake on the Old Allatoona Road, and you will come to the Allatoona Pass Battlefield, a Georgia State Park. The parking lot will be on your left.*

GPS: N 34.11395, W 84.71499

## Stop 1 - At Allatoona Pass

The Allatoona Pass Battlefield is maintained as a part of Red Top Mountain State Park near Emerson, Georgia. A parking lot is provided beside the old railroad bed that once made its way through the deep cut in the Allatoona Mountains. From the parking area, a trail network offers several ways to visit the site today.

One trail makes its way north through the old railroad cut, following the route that the Great Locomotive chase occurred over. It was the route used by both armies to send countless[(wlw)] carloads of ammunition and other supplies to the armies fighting in Tennessee, around Chattanooga, or, when in Union hands, to supply Sherman in the final stages of his Atlanta campaign. Other trails take you onto the heights to see the remains of the once formidable Union fortifications.

Today, interpretive markers tell the story of the garrison as well as the battle of October 5, 1864. From the remains of the Star Fort, an appreciation for the challenging terrain is readily gained, and it is possible to imagine what it was like for the defenders that day as they endured assault after assault from French's desperate Missourians, Texans, and Mississippians.

### ➤ TO STOP 2

*Turn off of I-75 at Exit 320 at Resaca, Georgia. Turn east onto highway 136 and continue over the railroad tracks to the Fort Wayne Civil War Historic Site; turn right onto Taylor Ridge Road to reach the graveled parking lot for the Fort.*

GPS: N 34.58282, W 84.93831

## Stop 2 - At Resaca

You now stand amidst what was once a large Union fortification complex that had cannibalized the small Confederate redoubt that had once stood atop the hill south of your location.

Today the Fort Wayne Civil War Historic Site encompasses 65 acres and is maintained by Gordon County. A complex system

(wlw)

of trenches and other fortifications was constructed to protect the critical railroad bridge over the Oostanaula River after the capture of the town in May of 1864. A trail will take you through the interior of the heavy fortifications. It's easy to get a sense of the site's strength and understand why the Union garrison, though greatly outnumbered, stood up boldly to Hood's demand for surrender.

### ➤ TO STOP 3

*Off I-75 at Exit 333, turn east onto Walnut Avenue and make your way to downtown Dalton; turn left onto North Glennwood Drive, and proceed to Fort Hill Circle; turn right and proceed up the hill toward Morris Innovative High School. Be aware that the site of the Fort sits on property that is now a functioning high school; parking can be found along Fort Hill Circle.*

GPS: N 34.772252, W 84.963508

## Stop 3 - At Dalton

From these heights, the garrison of Dalton witnessed the deployment of the Army of Tennessee to the west, south, and north of their fort. Today, interpretive markers tell the story of the USCT garrison and the events of that fateful October afternoon that witnessed the end of their quest for freedom. Unlike their comrades at Resaca, there were no reinforcements and no series of complex fortifications to aide them in presenting a ruse. Instead, fear of a repeat of Fort Pillow led Colonel Johnson to surrender his garrison and risk the consequences. Little remains of the Confederate positions, although a portion of the army's artillery was deployed along the edge of what is today Whitfield Memorial Gardens due east of your position on South Ridge Street.

## → TO STOP 4

*This site is atop Taylor's Ridge at Maddox Gap (the historic Shipp's Gap) off highway 136 near the West Armuchee community. Parking is provided along the side of the road at the historic wayside atop Taylor's Ridge.*

GPS: N 34.690571, W 85.188244

## Stop 4 – At Shipp's Gap

Just to the south of you, the 24th South Carolina deployed behind a stone wall along the military crest of the ridge, facing east toward West Armuchee Valley, where they could see the deployment of what seemed to be countless Union soldiers. Ultimately, the fight here was an extremely one-sided affair with a large portion of the 24th being captured in an advanced post on a knoll just to the east of you. After the retreat of what remained of the South Carolinians, General Sherman established his headquarters on these heights as he tried to figure out where Hood was headed and what his objective truly was.

(wlw)

## → TO STOP 5

*There is no direct route from Shipp's Gap to Decatur, making directions intricate and complicated. Use a GPS or map app to plot out the best route.*

GPS: N 34.614313, W 86.98365419999999

## Stop 5 – In Decatur, Alabama

Today, not much remains of the battlefield of Decatur, but a walking trail around the downtown area—The Decatur Civil War Walking Tour—will take you to several spots that can give you a taste of the fighting that did occur along the banks of the Tennessee River. A series of interpretive plaques help tell the story today. The walking tour begins at the Decatur Convention and Visitors Bureau.

## ⟶ TO STOP 6

*From downtown Decatur make your way to Hwy 31, turning left to travel north until it merges with Alt Hwy 72. Crossing the Tennessee River, continue on 72 until the interchange with Interstate 65. Take the on ramp onto I-65 North and continue on to the exit 53, which will place you on Rt. 396. Travel west on 396 until you come to Kedron Road. Take a left and continue on Kedron until the intersection with Denning Lane. Turn right onto Denning and continue onto Oaklawn.*

GPS: N 35.7218659, W 86.92938570000001

### Stop 6 - At Oaklawn

Begin your tour of Spring Hill at the gate in front of Oaklawn off of Denning Lane. Oaklawn can be viewed to the north and is on private property; do not trespass. Here, General Hood established his headquarters on the fateful evening of November 29, 1864. From here sprang much of the controversy that still haunts the history of the Tennessee campaign. Just east of you, the flanking column of the Army of Tennessee made its way northward and, in the fields to the north, the divisions deployed and moved westward—although, for various reasons, none would strike their objective, the Columbia Turnpike.

## ⟶ TO STOP 7

*Make your way eastward on Denning Lane a short distance to the intersection with Kedron Road (Rally Hill Pike), and turn left proceeding northward along the route, crossing under Saturn Parkway and arriving at the parking lot for the Spring Hill battlefield.*

GPS: N 35.7218659, W 86.92938570000001

### Stop 7 - At Spring Hill Battlefield

The slope of the hill before you is the only significant portion of the Spring Hill site that preserves an area where combat occurred. General Mark Lowrey's Alabamans and Mississippians deployed here just off the Rally Hill Turnpike and began to advance toward the setting autumn sun. As they moved over the crest of the hill in front of you, they discovered that a portion of Col. Luther Bradley's brigade deployed along the edge of the woods to your front and firing into their flank. This proved to be a critical moment: Lowrey deployed his command to deal with this threat, which caused him to divert his men from their original objective. He was soon joined by the rest of Cleburne's division, which routed Bradley's brigade. The retreating Federals made their way north and westward from the crest of this hill down into the low ground and branch you see to the north, with Cleburne's men in pursuit as precious daylight slipped away. A walking tour of the site will help you gain a better understanding of the events that played out here.

(wlw)

## ➤ TO STOP 8

*Turn left and continue north into Spring Hill on Kedron Road to the intersection with U.S. Highway 31/Main Street and turn right; proceed to Van Dorn Drive, and turn into the drive.*

GPS: N 35.748056, W 86.931667

## Stop 8 – At Martin Cheairs's Home

Before you is Martin Cheairs's Home, which was being used by Maj. Gen. David Stanley as his headquarters during the Spring Hill affair. Earlier, it was the site of the murder of controversial Confederate General Earl Van Dorn. A nearby wayside tells the story of that Spring Hill affair. On this high ground, the Union artillery was deployed facing southward, blunting the pursuit of Cleburne's men after the route of Bradley's command.

(wlw)

## ➤ TO STOP 9

*Turn back south and proceed down Highway 31 to the entrance to Rippavilla Plantation. Turn left and follow the gravel road to the parking lot. Once parked, make your way northward across the graveled drive, and follow the trail in front of you out into the open field.*

GPS: N 35.7318599, W 86.9538071

## Stop 9 – At Rippavilla Plantation

(wlw)

In these fields—just a few yards from the Columbia Turnpike—Hood's great opportunity was lost as the men of his army made bivouac here. Farther to the north, in the growing darkness of the night of November 29, Schofield's men made their way northward.

Today you can see how close the sides were. Imagine the cars and trucks you see headed north were the wagons and columns of Schofield's regiments, and you can see how close Hood came to victory here.

Return to the parking lot and make your way into the visitor center for Rippavilla. Many stories are associated with this home, an example of the palatial magnificence that so awed many of Hood's men as they entered the region. The house was also the site of the mysterious meeting Hood had with some of his generals on the morning of November 30, and it's from here that the march to Franklin and destiny began.

## → TO STOP 10

*Turn right and proceed up U.S. Highway 31 toward Franklin. As you travel northward, note the rolling landscape and patches of cedar that are a hallmark of the Middle Tennessee region. Upon approach to Franklin, you will see the line of hills that marked the south end of the Franklin battlefield.*

*Continue north, passing the Winstead Hill Park, and turn right onto Mark C. Hatcher Memorial Parkway. Proceed to Business 431, and turn left. Continue on to the entrance to the Eastern Flank Battlefield Park.*

GPS: N 35.90417, W 86.857778

## Stop 10 – At Eastern Flank Battlefield Park, Visitor Center

Proceed down the drive to the parking lot for the visitor center and begin your tour inside it. You can, at this time, also purchase tickets to tour Carnton House, but it is advised that you save the house tour for your last stop.

**Carnton as it appears today belies the horror of the field hospital that covered every inch of it on the night of November 30th.** (wlw)

## → TO STOP 11

*After viewing the exhibits at the visitor center, return to your car and return to Business 431. Turn right and proceed to Mark C. Hatcher Memorial Parkway; turn right and travel to the intersection with U.S. Highway 31; turn left and then turn left again into the parking lot for Winstead Hill Park.*

GPS: N 35.531924, W 86.523994

(wlw)

## Stop 11 - At Winstead Hill Park

(wlw)

From the parking lot, follow the trail that will bring you to an overlook from which you can view the Franklin battlefield. Though heavily developed today, you can still see the rolling terrain over which the Army of Tennessee made its attack on the late afternoon of November 30, 1864. You can also imagine the last meeting that occurred near here with Hood and his generals and what crossed their minds.

Over this hill, Cheatham's corps rolled forward like a tidal wave, deploying in the low ground before you to make last-minute preparations. Around 4 p.m., a signal was sent from the top of this hill, and the attack began.

As you make your way down the hill, take Generals' Walk to view a series of monuments erected for the Confederate generals killed in the battle.

(wlw)

## → TO STOP 12

*Turn left, being careful of the traffic, and proceed north along Business 31 (Columbia Avenue) toward downtown Franklin. This drive emulates the advance of the Confederates; you will pass the private property that is Privett Knoll and then pass a historic marker that designates the positions of Wagner's advanced line. As you proceed, remember that, in 1864, both sides of the road here were large expanses of open fields. Continue on to West Fowlkes Street and turn left; travel a short distance and the parking lot for the Carter House is on your left.*

GPS: N 35.91528, W 86.87278

## *Stop 12 - At the Carter House*

The Carter House Visitor Center offers a video and exhibits that tell the story of the property (as well as the diorama that spurred the author's interest in the battle when he was a child!). A tour of the Carter House will give you the story of a family confronted with the horrors of the war, but afterwards, take time to explore the grounds on your own.

Take note of the bullet-marked buildings and imagine the horrific hand-to-hand fighting that swirled in the yard around you. Also take a moment to look out over the reconstructed second line of works toward the main line that ran along Strahl Street in front of you.

Go to the other side of the Carters' garden and imagine the charge of Smith's brigade, bringing Tod Carter home and to his death. Sadness emanates here but so does courage. The men of the 44th Missouri defended this area and, although no one initially thought much of the 183rd Ohio, those green troops proved their worth here and became veterans on this ground.

Walk to the east side of Columbia Avenue, being careful about the traffic, and onto the recently reclaimed cotton gin property. A decade ago, this was a strip mall and homes; now you can view the angling trench line and the site of the cotton gin. Here, some of the most horrific combat of the entire war occurred. Imagine the sounds of the battle here—the barking of Harvey of the 104th Ohio and the sight of the onrushing Confederates. Take a few minutes to explore, and then make your way back to the sidewalk along Columbia Avenue and walk northward past the Carter House to the Lotz House.

The Lotz House also witnessed the swirling tide of battle as Opdycke's men surged forward to help seal the fate of Hood's attack. Near here, the 175th Ohio and

the Southern Unionists of the 16th and 12th Kentucky and 8th Tennessee charged into the melee around between the gin and turnpike, driving back the veterans of Cleburne's division. A visit to the Lotz House will give another story of a family impacted by war and another witness to the fighting of 1864 and its aftermath.

Return to the Carter House and spend a few more minutes walking the grounds before returning to your car.

## ⟶ TO STOP 13

*Turn left onto Columbia Avenue and proceed into downtown Franklin. Turn right onto 3rd Avenue, which becomes Route 96 (The Murfreesboro Road). Continue on until the intersection with Eddy Lane, then turn left on Eddy Lane, and proceed, following the signs to the parking area for Fort Granger on your left.*

GPS: N 35.92611, W 86.85917

### *Stop 13 - At Fort Granger*

Fort Granger was constructed in the spring of 1863 as Gen. William S. Rosecrans—then commander of the Army of the Cumberland—worked to protect the right flank of his army, which was centered on Murfreesboro. The fort was named after Gen. Gordon Granger, one of Rosecrans's corps commanders who later played a prominent role in the battles at Chickamauga and Chattanooga. In June of 1865, while commanding forces in Texas, Granger would send out word of the end of slavery into the Texas interior, leading to the establishment of the Juneteenth Holiday. Granger had seen little combat until 1864, when the guns of Battery G, 1st Ohio, added the fury into the flank of Stewart's attack.

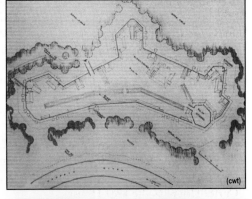

(cwt)

(wlw)

Positioned in the south end of the fort, a platform allows visitors to view the area and get an idea of why, besides the safety of the position, Schofield relocated his headquarters here. The view to the south and west, much more open in 1864, gave him a front-row seat to the deploying Confederate forces and the early part of the battle. Explore the fort. Signs point out the different parts of the fort and give an idea of the heavy defenses.

## ➤ TO STOP 14

*Return to Eddy Lane, turn right, and continue back to Route 96. Turn right, and proceed back toward downtown. When you come to South Margin Street, turn left and then turn onto Lewisburg Avenue, following the signs toward Carnton. Once you reach the entrance to the Eastern Flank Battlefield, turn in again and make your way to the parking lot.*

GPS: N 35.90417, W 86.857778

*Stop 14 – At Eastern Flank Battlefield; fieldwalk*

You are now on the largest piece of the Franklin battlefield that remains undeveloped. There is a walking tour of the property, but it is recommended to walk back toward the entrance and find the wayside about the advance of Scott's Brigade. Follow these signs along the edge of the property, and you are now walking in the footsteps of one of the ill-fated Confederate brigades as it advanced over the fields of Carnton Plantation. From along this route artillery posted on the high ground behind the Union defenses to your front began to pound Loring's men. The story of Scott's brigade can be, in part, (wlw)

viewed as representative of many other commands on the field that day.

At the edge of the property, a sign will tell about the rest of the advance. Later, you can also drive back to the Collins Farm Property, which is closer to town and witness to some of the final scenes of the charge near the railroad cut and Osage orange hedge. At this time, however, proceed back to Carnton for the house tour (using those tickets purchased earlier) and to hear the story of the aftermath of the battle.

Carnton House witnessed the advance of Stewart's corps as it swarmed around the house and its grounds, but in the aftermath of the fighting, it became a field hospital and a witness to the great suffering that occurred. Bloodstains are still

visible in many rooms of the house and on its back porch. Here Cleburne's, Strahl's, and Granbury's bodies were brought and laid beside one another. Adams was also probably brought here, as well as several staff officers. If walls could talk, these would tell stories you might not want to hear.

After you have toured the house, make your way to the nearby Confederate Cemetery and view the expense of battle. Here are interned around 1,500 of the dead of the Army of Tennessee, of which only 780 are known. Walk among the stones and you will almost feel the high cost of the attack. You will see headstones and markers bearing the names of many officers, and you will see the staggering losses of the Missouri brigade. No more fitting place to end a tour of Franklin can be found than here—the ultimate cost of the battle lies all around you.

# Confederate Artillery at Franklin

## APPENDIX A

The story of the battle of Franklin from the Confederate point of view has always been one about the infantry. As the common telling goes, Hood ordered his frontal assault without waiting for any of his artillery to arrive.

The bulk of the artillery was with Lt. Gen. S. D. Lee in the rear of Hood's column, although several batteries did make it onto the field to play some role in the fighting. While they did not play a major factor, they did endure and sacrifice like their infantry counterparts and thus, in some ways, have been unsung participants in the battle.

Artillerymen were present as detachments without their own guns, sent along with the flanking column to Spring Hill; there they were expected to man guns that Confederates expected to capture. Similar detached units also accompanied a handful of batteries in each corps, such as Douglas's Texas Battery that accompanied Cheatham.

The most graphic account, though, can be found from the gunners of Guibor's Missouri Battery that went in with Stewart's division. The battery was broken up into sections and moved along at intervals during the attack. What follows are the harrowing first-person accounts of Franklin from a couple of "red legs" perspectives:

### Gunner Samuel Dunlap:
*Our section was ordered to go out in front of the advance line & commence firing. We were soon in position-guns loaded, & at the command fire! sent two shells screaming through the air in the direction of the fortified little city.*

*This was a signal for our men to prepare for a charge all around the lines—& a deafening roar of artillery—attended with the bursting of shells & whizzing of minnies—from the enemies guns, was heard in return. Our pieces fire as rapidly as possible & until our first line of battle passed—then limbered up—fell in their*

**Artillery at Winstead Hill Park overlooks the battlefield from the Confederate perspective.** (cm)

*rear to join in the charge. This was the first & only instance during the war in which we were ordered to charge as artillery—but Hood's intention on this occasion was to take everything by storm—& had he been successful—when a good position for artillery had been reached—we would have been ready to plant our guns. Our advance extended down an open field, over a small ravine & railroad—up an inclined plain in full view of the enemy. Our horses had become almost wild with excitement—rearing & pitching to free themselves from their drivers—& escape the 'hailstorm' of shot & shell, what was tearing up the ground around them.*

*In crossing the railroad, one of the wheel tugs on my gun broke which necessitated a short halt. . . . We had moved but a few paces from where the breakage occurred—when the same wheel driver (Stubbs) was hit on the head with a fragment of shell—& fell forward between his horses—lodging upon the bridle reins and end of pole. He was born from the field & place filled by one of the cannoniers. We succeeded in driving the enemy from their first & second line of works but our first line of battle becoming so decimated by the continuous hail of shell, grape, canister & minnies into their ranks—had to be filled by the second & third. Not being able to obtain a position, from which we could do execution, without endangering the lives of our own men-the battery was halted at the first line of works—but our infantry kept steadily on-on! until their enemy was driven behind the last line of entrenchments. We were told to remain in place, subject to orders—& I assure you the continual rain of shot, shell & the sight of our comrades falling around us-made our position anything but a pleasant one. To be a silent & helpless spectator, when death in all its horridness, is hovering over you—listen to the cries of the wounded & dying as they are being carted off the field-requires greater nerve—than to face the cannons mouth in heat of battle.*

As the fighting finally died down at about 9 p.m., the guns were ordered back a short distance for the night. Gunners were awakened again at 3 a.m., and as the bulk of the army's artillery arrived on the field, they were ordered into position to bombard the Federal positions—but come dawn, they discovered the positions had been abandoned.

## Gunner W. L. Truman, Guibor's Battery:

*My battery (Guibore's) was ordered to follow Loring's division and we followed close behind Loring's line of battle, on his extreme right, close to the Harpeth river, not more than thirty feet from the stream at times. The opposite was a dense forest all the way to the Franklin pike, and not a one of the enemy to be seen. It looked to me to be but an hours work to throw a bridge across that narrow stream and rush a few brigades through that timber to the pike in the rear of the enemy.*

*The ground over which Loring's and Walthall's divisions advanced to the charge, was sparely timbered and well set in bluegrass, free of all undergrowth and I could see our line for at least a half mile as it advanced to a common center. It was an inspiring sight. The enemy's artillery fire on our center and left was heavy, but on our right, at least in front of Gen. Loring's division, had only one battery playing upon it, and that was on the enemy's extreme left, near the river. It was well handled and did considerable execution, one shell bursted right in the midst of our line, as it moved forward in front of our battery, and perhaps as many as ten men fell in a heap, two of them raised themselves up on their hands and then fell back and all was still in death. The line on either side of the gap never quivered or lost step, nor turned their heads to look back, but pressed on as if nothing had happened, and the line was soon closed. We were*

(wlw)

*within easy musket range of the battery, but were not allowed to fire a shot. We cannoneers inquired, and clamored for a chance to return the fire and protect our infantry, but our officers told us that Gen Hood had given orders that no artillery should be used as the women and children were all in the town. And as far up the line as I could see, there was not a shot fired, from any of our batteries, and yet we were kept under fire during the battle.*

*As our line of battle drew near the enemy's works, I saw their picket line leave their hiding places and make a rush for their main works and when safely inside, a sheet of fire belched forth from the enemy's breastworks as far around the semicircle as I could see, then our line went forward on a run in almost perfect order, for quite a distance without firing a gun. The sheet of fire like long flashes of lightning continued to play in the midst of the smoking volcano of death, in their front and the enemy's battery upon their left redoubled its efforts of destruction.*

*Suddenly the Confederate line came to a halt, almost as it seemed to me at the edge of the blazing, smoking breastworks and fired a volley or two, and then the whole line wheeled and made a rush for the rear and as the hailstorm of lead and cannister followed them, 'they ran because they could not fly.' When out of range of the volleys of musketry, every man halted of his own accord and our line of battle was soon in perfect order again. Our men were old soldiers, heroes of a hundred battles, well drilled and knew their duty and were never panic stricken, when ordered or forced to retire from the face of the enemy. It was so in this case, no effort was made to return to the assault on our right, so far as I could see, I knew there was a good cause for it. Something more than the presence of the enemy inside of their works, which was bad enough, but did not learn the real facts until I investigated myself early the next morning*

*The battle seemed to be general all around the town, the cannonading was incessant to our left and center, and the musketry fearful at times. I had heard nothing like it except at Corinth and Gen Bowen's charge with his division at Baker's Creek. Darkness was soon upon us yet the battle continued with great obstinacy at many points until late at night. My battery had halted within range of the minie balls, while the line went forward in the charge and we never moved from that place during the night. Our horses were not unharnessed or fed. It was a real sad disappointment to the officers and men of our battery, to quietly look upon that Federal battery doing its deadly work in perfect safety. Our gunners were splendid marksmen as they had practiced until they could place a shell in a few minutes just where they wanted it, and felt sure that if they could not silence that battery, they could so cripple it in a few minutes that it could not harm our men.*

While playing only a limited role in the fight, the artillery branch was represented in the fighting at Franklin—a fight that was an artillery hell of a different sort.

# The Lost Banners

## APPENDIX B

One of the greatest testimonies of the fierceness of the fighting at Franklin appears in the number of battle flags that were captured from the Confederate forces. The Army of Tennessee lost at least 22 flags in the fighting there—more than they had ever lost in battle before.

One unknown brigade marker flag
1st Alabama Infantry
16th Alabama Infantry
33rd Alabama Infantry
50th Alabama Infantry
6th Arkansas Infantry
5th and 13th (Consolidated) Arkansas Infantry
1st and 3rd (Consolidated) Florida Infantry
32nd Mississippi Infantry
3rd Mississippi Infantry
15th Mississippi Infantry
22nd Mississippi Infantry
32nd Mississippi Infantry
33rd Mississippi Infantry
1st Missouri Cavalry (Dismounted)
1st and 4th Missouri (Consolidated) Infantry
2nd and 6th Missouri (Consolidated) Infantry
29th Tennessee Infantry
42nd Tennessee Infantry
53rd Tennessee Infantry

*Plus, two flags without unit designation, one from Cheatham's Corps and another from Stewart's Corps*

The Confederates snatched a smaller number of flags in their struggle along the line—just 12 from the various Union forces fought.

51st Illinois Infantry (recaptured)
72nd Illinois Infantry (both their Regimental and National Colors were lost)
107th Illinois Infantry
57th Indiana Infantry
97th Ohio Infantry
44th Missouri Infantry

*Plus, four from Army of the Ohio units and two from Army of the Cumberland units (all from Wagner's division)*

# *Preservation of Franklin*

## APPENDIX C

Franklin represents a remarkable preservation story—but it has been a long, hard road.

The destruction of the battlefield began shortly after the fighting ended because the land upon which the battle was fought was working farmland. The owners needed it to sustain their livelihood. The cotton gin was rebuilt by the Carters, but then torn down in the 1880s when the land it sat upon was sold. In 1887, the Battle Ground Academy was built at the corner of Cleburne Street and Columbia Avenue (the former Columbia Turnpike) in the area where Cleburne's division had charged. The construction saw the first monument on the field: a cenotaph to mark the spot where Cleburne's body was found after the battle.

By the early 1900s, as the first national military parks were established, supporters began to call to advocate for the establishment of a memorial park at Franklin. However, interest seemed to be mixed and funding was unavailable. The idea seemed to fade away as development began to claim more of the battlefield. Even the Cleburne cenotaph was torn down during this time. For several decades, the battle of Franklin passed from most people's memory.

As the nation approached the centennial of the Civil War in the 1950s, memory stirred. Bennett Hunter, then owner of the Carter House, deeded the house and the land it sat on to the State of Tennessee. That was in 1951; it was opened to the public in 1953. In 1958, the United Daughters of the Confederacy received the property at Winstead Hill as a donation. They cared for the property until 1982, when they deeded the land to the Sons of Confederate Veterans.

A Pizza Hut that sat at the center of the battlefield became the symbol for battlefield preservation at Franklin. Its demolition, and the subsequent reclamation of the property, has been one of the great success stories of the preservation movement. (js/abt)

Things remained quiet for several decades. Then, in 1971 the city purchased Fort Granger, and in 1977, Carnton Plantation was deeded to the Carnton Association. Along with Winstead Hill and Carter House, that made

While most preservation battles focus on saving land, Franklin has seen dramatic success in actual battlefield reclamation. Preservationists have reclaimed battlefield property and demolished modern structures to restore the landscape to its wartime appearance. (sh/abt)(sh/abt)

three landmarks open to the public and established focal points where all future preservation efforts would connect.

In 1989, the approach of the 125th anniversary of the battle spurred renewed interest, and Save the Franklin Battlefield was formed. The group began with efforts to help the existing sites while also looking at a long-term plan to "reclaim" portions of the battlefield. By then, Franklin was a poster child for a lost battlefield. The Pizza Hut that sat upon the site of Cleburne's cenotaph became one of the most frequently seen images in the burgeoning Civil War preservation movement.

The preservation efforts bore fruit in 2001 when Collins Farm—a three-acre site near the railroad where Loring's men had suffered so much—was acquired. Another ally appeared in 2005 in the form of Franklin's Charge, an organization that consolidated the preservation efforts of other groups in the area. Since then, Franklin has seen a nearly continuous stream of reclamation victories—the hallmark of which was the purchase of the Pizza Hut and its subsequent demolition.

Following that victory, a block of buildings along Columbia Avenue and the houses located on the site of the Gin House were purchased and demolished, leaving the scene of some of the worst

fighting clean of modern developments. "Preserving the missing piece of this puzzle removed the last obstacle to creating a contiguous park allowing visitors to reflect on one of the Civil War's bloodiest episodes," the Civil War Trust said in a media statement.

The biggest victory to date was the purchase of the country club adjacent to the Carnton Property, a total of 112 acres, which became known as the "Eastern Flank Battlefield." It was a cooperative effort by Franklin's Charge, The Civil War Trust, and the City of Franklin.

As of this writing, preservation work at Franklin continues as more adjacent properties are purchased and added to that land already protected. If one is searching for a successful story of preservation, one need only look at the good work in Franklin, Tennessee.

Land preservation and restoration continues at Franklin, where small parcels—such as the greenspace next to the Carter house grounds—command high prices because of market values. (cm)

# Memories of Franklin

## APPENDIX D

My interest in the American Civil War stretches back to my first visits to the Chickamauga Battlefield, where I now work telling its stories. However, as a child, my interest in history was nurtured and encouraged by my Aunt Elaine. She was a retired schoolteacher, and though she never had any children, she and her husband, James, somewhat adopted me. They began taking me on trips they took to places like Cowpens, Stones River, and Franklin.

My first memory of Franklin was the diorama in the visitor center at the Carter House. I remember running up to it and pressing my nose against the glass to view the plastic soldiers battling to the death along their entrenchments of reddened something or other. That visit lit the spark for my interest in that battle—the bullet holes in the Carter House buildings, the diorama, the old uniforms—it all worked together.

Soon, I was no longer the boy from William Faulkner's Intruder in the Dust. For this Southern boy, it wasn't July 3rd but November 30th, and it wasn't the orders for Pickett's Advance, it was the one for Cleburne's.

As the years went by, I continued to visit Franklin. The older I got and the more I read about the battle, the more the place saddened me—not only because of the tragic losses there, but also from seeing that so little of the field existed still. Sadly, it became a warped game for me to drive from my home in North Georgia to Franklin, going through Murfreesboro, and seeing how much had been developed since my last visit.

A monument marking the location where Patrick Cleburne's body was found was placed near the Columbia Turnpike decades after the battle. The monument was later removed. The monument there today is a reproduction of the original. (cm)

But in the mid 1990s, that began to change. Now, on each visit to Franklin, more of the land is newly free from the modern development that once obscured the stage of the great November drama.

I also became acquainted with many of the historians in the town—men such as Thomas Cartright, who took the time to share with me his knowledge of the battle, as did others. Over the years, I began to read and research more about the battle. I first took a strong interest, in the early '90s, when reading Wiley Sword's Embrace an Angry Wind, a book that I have read many times over. As I read more, I came to disagree with Wiley's story, particularly in regard to General Hood, but I still think it is a wonderfully written book. It still sits worn and without its dust jacket on my bookshelf alongside others about the campaign.

I came to see the battle in a different light, though. It was not simply an all-out frontal assault by the Confederate army, but a series of hammering blows, and though it was said to be a five-hour battle, most of the intense fighting and casualties were inflicted in a much shorter span. That was the genesis of this book.

My interest in the men on the other side grew, and though the story of the Confederates can sometimes eclipse that of the Union, it takes two sides to fight a battle. It now seems surreal to visit Franklin—to go there to speak to a group or to lead a tour on the campaign. I was once the kid wanting to know all about the fight, to learn its story. Now I am the one telling it. I just hope that I do the men of both sides justice.

No matter how you look at it, restoration of the Franklin battlefield has been a huge success story, opening up new understanding of the battle. (mt/abt) (mt/abt)

## NOVEMBER 30, 1864

### UNION FORCES
Maj. Gen. John M. Schofield

**FOURTH CORPS:** Maj. Gen. David Stanley
**FIRST DIVISION:** Brig. Gen. Nathan Kimball
**1st Brigade:** Col. Issac M. Kirby
*21st Illinois · 38th Illinois · 31st Indiana · 81st Indiana · 90th Ohio · 101st Ohio*

**2nd Brigade:** Brig. Gen. Walter Whitaker
*96th Illinois · 115th Illinois · 35th Indiana · 21st Kentucky · 23rd Kentucky
40th Ohio · 45th Ohio · 51st Ohio*

**3rd Brigade:** Brig. Gen. William Grose
*75th Illinois · 80th Illinois · 84th Illinois · 9th Indiana · 30th Indiana
36th Indiana · 84th Indiana · 77th Pennsylvania*

**SECOND DIVISION:** Brig. Gen. George Wagner
**1st Brigade:** Brig. Gen. Emerson Opdycke
*24th Wisconsin · 36th Illinois · 44th Illinois · 73rd Illinois · 74th-88th Illinois
125th Ohio*

**2nd Brigade:** Col. John Q. Lane
*100th Illinois · 40th Indiana · 57th Indiana · 28th Kentucky · 26th Ohio
97th Ohio*

**3rd Brigade:** Col. Joseph Conrad
*42nd Illinois · 51st Illinois · 79th Illinois · 15th Missouri · 64th Ohio · 65th Ohio*

**THIRD DIVISION:** Brig. Gen. Thomas J. Wood
**1st Brigade:** Col. Abel D. Streight
*89th Illinois · 51st Indiana · 8th Kansas · 15th Ohio · 49th Ohio*

**2nd Brigade:** Philip Sidney Post
*59th Illinois · 41st Ohio · 71st Ohio · 93rd Ohio · 124th Ohio*

**3rd Brigade:** Col. Frederick Knefler
*79th Indiana · 86th Indiana · 13th Ohio · 19th Ohio · 17th Kentucky*

**Fourth Corps Artillery:** Capt. Lyman Bridges
*Bridge's Illinois Battery · 1st Kentucky Battery · Battery A, 1st Ohio Light Artillery Battery G, 1st Ohio Light Artillery · 6th Ohio Battery · 20th Ohio Battery Battery M, 4th United States Light Artillery · Independent Battery Pennsylvania Light Artillery*

**TWENTY-THIRD CORPS:** Brig. Gen. Jacob Cox
**SECOND DIVISION:** Brig. Gen. Thomas Ruger
**Second Brigade:** Col. Orlando H. Moore
*107th Illinois · 80th Indiana · 129th Indiana · 23rd Michigan · 111th Ohio 118th Ohio*

**Third Brigade:** Col. Silas Strickland
*72nd Illinois · 44th Missouri · 50th Ohio · 183rd Ohio*

**THIRD DIVISION:** Brig. Gen. James W. Reilly
**1st Brigade:** Brig. Gen. James W. Reilly
*12th Kentucky · 16th Kentucky · 8th Tennessee · 100th Ohio · 104th Ohio*

**2nd Brigade:** Col. John S. Casement
*65th Illinois · 65th Indiana · 124th Indiana · 103rd Ohio · 5th Tennessee*

**3rd Brigade:** Col. Israel Stiles
*112th Illinois · 63rd Indiana · 120th Indiana · 128th Indiana*

**CAVALRY CORPS:** Maj. Gen. James H. Wilson
**FIRST DIVISION:** Brig. Gen. Edward M. McCook
**1st Brigade:** Brig. Gen. John T. Croxton
*4th Kentucky Mounted Infantry · 8th Iowa · 2nd Michigan · 1st Tennessee*

**FIFTH DIVISION:** Brig. Gen. Edward Hatch
**1st Brigade:** Col. Robert R. Stewart
*3rd Illinois · 11th Indiana*

**2nd Brigade:** Col. Datus E. Coon
*12th Tennessee · 2nd Iowa · 6th Illinois · 7th Illinois · 9th Illinois*

**SIXTH DIVISION:** Brig. Gen. Richard W. Johnson
**1st Brigade:** Col. Thomas J. Harrison
*5th Iowa · 7th Ohio · 16th Illinois*

**2nd Brigade:** Col. James Biddle
*3rd Tennessee · 6th Indiana · 8th Michigan · 14th Illinois*

## CONFEDERATE FORCES: ARMY OF TENNESSEE
Lt. Gen. John Bell Hood

**CHEATHAM'S CORPS:** Maj. Gen. Benjamin Franklin Cheatham
**CHEATHAM'S DIVISION:** Maj. Gen. John C. Brown
**Maney's Brigade:** Brig. Gen. John C. Carter
*1st-27th Tennessee · 4th (34th) Tennessee (Provisional)-6th-9th-50th Tennessee
8th-16th-28th Tennessee*

**Gist's Brigade:** Brig. Gen. States Rights Gist
*16th South Carolina · 24th South Carolina · 2nd Georgia Battalion Sharpshooters 46th
Georgia · 8th Georgia Battalion-65th Georgia*

**Gordon's Brigade:** Brig. Gen. George Washington Gordon
*11th-29th Tennessee · 12th-47th Tennessee · 154th Tennessee
13th-51st-52nd Tennessee*

**Strahl's Brigade:** Brig. Gen. Otho F. Strahl
*4th-5th -33rd-38thTennessee · 19th -41st Tennessee · 24th Tennessee · 31st Tennessee*

**CLEBURNE'S DIVISION:** Maj. Gen. Patrick R. Cleburne
**Govan's Brigade:** Brig. Gen. Daniel C. Govan
*1st-15th Arkansas · 2nd-24th Arkansas · 5th-13th Arkansas · 6th-7th Arkansas
8th-19th Arkansas · 3rd Confederate*

**Granbury's Brigade:** Brig. Gen. Hiram B. Granbury
*7th Texas · 6th-15th Texas · 10th Texas · 17th-18th Texas · 24th-25th Texas
5th Confederate*

**Lowrey's Brigade:** Brig. Gen. Mark P. Lowrey
*16th-33rd-45th Alabama · 3rd Mississippi Battalion-5th Mississippi · 8th Mississippi-
32nd Mississippi*

**BATE'S DIVISION:** Maj. Gen. William B. Bate
**Smith's Brigade:** Brig. Gen. Thomas Benton Smith
*2nd-10th-20th-37th Tennessee · 15th-30th Tennessee · 4th Georgia Battalion Sharpshooters
· 37th Georgia*

**Jackson's Brigade:** Brig. Gen. Henry Rootes Jackson
*1st Confederate Georgia · 1st Battalion Georgia Sharpshooters · 25th Georgia
29th-30th Georgia · 66th Georgia*

**Finley's Brigade:** Col. Robert Bullock
*1st Florida Cavalry (Dismounted)-4th Florida · 1st-3rd Florida · 6th Florida
7th Florida*

**CHEATHAM'S CORPS ARTILLERY:** Col. Melancthon Smith
**Hotchkiss's Battalion:**
*Bledsoe's Missouri Battery   ·   Goldthwaite's Alabama Battery   ·   Helena Light Artillery (Key's Arkansas Battery)*

**Hoxton's Battalion:**
*Perry's Florida Battery   ·   Phelan's Alabama Battery   ·   Turner's Mississippi Battery*

**Cobb's Battalion:**
*Ferguson's South Carolina Battery   ·   Phillip's Tennessee Battery   ·   5th Company Washington Artillery (Louisiana)*

**LEE'S CORPS:** Lt. Gen. Stephen D. Lee
**JOHNSON'S DIVISION:** Maj. Gen. Edward Johnson
**Manigault's Brigade:** Brig. Gen. Arthur M. Manigault
*10th South Carolina   ·   19th South Carolina   ·   24th Alabama   ·   28th Alabama 34th Alabama*

**Deas's Brigade:** Brig. Gen. Zachariah C. Deas
*19th Alabama   ·   22nd Alabama   ·   25th Alabama   ·   39th Alabama 26th-50th Alabama*

**Sharp's Mississippi Brigade:** Brig. Gen. Jacob H. Sharp
*7th-9th Mississippi   ·   41st Mississippi   ·   9th Mississippi Battalion Sharpshooters-10th-44th Mississippi*

**Brantley's Brigade:** Brig. Gen. William F. Brantley
24th-34th Mississippi   ·   27th Mississippi   ·   29th-30th Mississippi

**CLAYTON'S DIVISION:** Maj. Gen. Henry D. Clayton
**Stovall's Brigade:** Brig. Gen. Marcellus A. Stovall
*40th Georgia   ·   41st Georgia   ·   42nd Georgia   ·   43rd Georgia   ·   52nd Georgia*

**Gibson's Brigade:** Brig. Gen. Randall Lee Gibson
*1st Louisiana Regulars   ·   4th Louisiana Battalion   ·   13th Louisiana   ·   14th Louisiana Battalion Sharpshooters   ·   16th Louisiana   ·   19th Louisiana   ·   20th Louisiana 25th Louisiana   ·   30th Louisiana*

**Holtzclaw's Brigade:** Brig. Gen. James H. Holtzclaw
*18th Alabama   ·   36th Alabama   ·   38th Alabama   ·   32nd-58th Alabama*

**STEVENSON'S DIVISION:** Maj. Gen. Carter L. Stevenson
**Cumming's Brigade:** Col. Elihu P. Watkins
*39th Georgia   ·   34th Georgia   ·   36th Georgia   ·   56th Georgia*

**Pettus's Brigade:** Brig. Gen. Edmund W. Pettus
*20th Alabama  ·  23rd Alabama  ·  30th Alabama  ·  31st Alabama  ·  46th Alabama*

**Palmer's Brigade:** Brig. Gen. Joseph B. Palmer
*3rd-18th Tennessee  ·  26th-45th Tennessee  ·  32nd Tennessee  ·  60th North Carolina*
*54th Virginia  ·  63rd Virginia*

**LEE'S CORPS ARTILLERY:** Maj. John W. Johnston
**Courtney's Battalion:**
*Dent's Alabama Battery  ·  Douglas's Texas Battery  ·  Garrity's Alabama Battery*

**Eldridge's Battalion:**
*Eufaula Light Artillery (Alabama)  ·  Fenner's Louisiana Battery  ·  Stanford's Mississippi Battery*

**Johnston's Battalion:**
*Cherokee Light Artillery (Van Den Corput's Georgia Battery)  ·  Marshall's Tennessee Battery*
*Stephens's Light Artillery*

**STEWART'S CORPS:** Lt. Alexander Peter Stewart
**LORING'S DIVISION:** Maj. Gen. William Wing Loring
**Adam's Brigade:** Brig. Gen. John Adams
*6th Mississippi  ·  14th Mississippi  ·  15th Mississippi  ·  20th Mississippi*
*23rd Mississippi  ·  43rd Mississippi*

**Featherston's Brigade:** Brig. Gen. Winfield Scott Featherston
*1st Battalion Mississippi Sharpshooters  ·  1st Mississippi  ·  3rd Mississippi*
*22nd Mississippi  ·  31st Mississippi  ·  33rd Mississippi  ·  40th Mississippi*

**Scott's Brigade:** Brig. Gen. Thomas M. Scott
*12th Louisiana  ·  27th-35th-49th Alabama  ·  55th Alabama  ·  57th Alabama*

**WALTHALL'S DIVISION:** Maj. Gen. Edward C. Walthall
**Quarles's Brigade:** Brig. Gen. William A. Quarles
*1st Alabama  ·  42nd Tennessee  ·  46th Tennessee  ·  49th Tennessee  ·  53rd Tennessee*
*55th Tennessee*

**Cantey's Brigade:** Brig. Gen. Charles M. Shelley
*17th Alabama  ·  26th Alabama  ·  29th Alabama  ·  37th Mississippi*

**Reynolds's Brigade:** Brig. Gen. Daniel H. Reynolds
*1st Arkansas Mounted Rifles  ·  2nd Arkansas Mounted Rifles  ·  4th Arkansas Battalion-4th*
*Arkansas-31st Arkansas  ·  9th Arkansas  ·  25th Arkansas*

**FRENCH'S DIVISION:** Maj. Gen. Samuel G. French
**Cockrell's Brigade:** Brig. Gen. Francis Marion Cockrell
*1st-4th Missouri   ·   2nd-6th Missouri   ·   3rd-5th Missouri   ·   1st Missouri Cavalry (Dismounted)-3rd Missouri Cavalry (Dismounted)*

**Sears's Mississippi Brigade:** Brig. Gen. Claudius W. Sears
*4th Mississippi   ·   7th Mississippi Battalion   ·   35th Mississippi   ·   46th Mississippi 36th Mississippi   ·   39th Mississippi*

**STEWART'S CORPS ARTILLERY:** Lt. Col. Samuel C. Williams
**Myrick's Battalion:**
*Bouanchard's Louisiana Battery   ·   Cowan's Mississippi Battery   ·   Darden's Mississippi Battery*

**Starr's Battalion:**
*Guibor's Missouri Battery   ·   Hoskin's Mississippi Battery   ·   Kolb's Alabama Battery*

**Truehart's Battalion:**
*Lumsden's Alabama Battery   ·   Selden's Alabama Battery   ·   Tarrant's Alabama Battery*

# Suggested Reading

*The Lost Papers of Confederate General John Bell Hood*
Stephen M. Hood
Savas Beatie (2015)
ISBN: 978-1611211825

One of the most important discoveries of recent Civil War historiography, the papers of General Hood cover more than just the Tennessee campaign, but do go a long way toward providing a better understanding of the events of November 29-30, 1864.

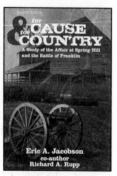

*For Cause and Country*
Eric A. Jacobson with Richard A. Rupp
O'More Publishing (2014)
ISBN: 978-0971744448

The definitive "must read" account of the battle of Franklin and the first modern study to incorporate current scholarship that has challenged the way we view the events that occurred on that late November afternoon.

*"Hood's Tennessee Campaign: From the Fall of Atlanta to the Battle of Franklin—Sept. 2 to Nov. 30, 1864."*
Eric A. Jacobson
*Blue & Gray* Magazine, 30, no. 4 (2014)
ISSN: 0741-2207

This very readable and informative guide from *Blue & Gray* covers the campaign up through the end of the battle.

*Hood's Tennessee Campaign*
James R. Knight
The History Press (2014)
ISBN: 978-1626195974

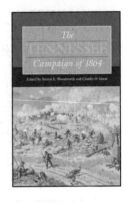

Another good general overview of the campaign, from its beginnings in Georgia to the retreat of Hood's forces from Tennessee in the aftermath of Nashville.

*The Tennessee Campaign of 1864 (Civil War Campaigns in the Heartland)*
Edited By Steven E. Woodworth and Charles D. Grear
Southern Illinois University Press (2016)
ISBN: 978-0809334520

A collection of essays on various aspects of the Tennessee Campaign as a whole, with notable entries including "The Long Lost Diary of Patrick R. Cleburne," "Killing at Franklin: Anatomy of Slaughter," and "The Destruction of the Army of Tennessee's Officer Corps at the Battle of Franklin." These can go a long way to helping a student of the battle gain a better understanding of the campaign.

*A Long and Bloody Task: The Atlanta Campaign, from Dalton to Kennesaw to the Chattahooche, May 5-July 18, 1864*
(Savas Beatie, 2016)

*All the Fighting They Want: The Atlanta Campaign, from Peachtree Creek to the Surrender of the City, July 18-September 2, 1864*
(Savas Beatie, 2017)

Steve Davis
ISBN-13: 978-1-61121-317-1
ISBN-13: 978-1-61121-319-5

The prelude to Hood's ill-fated Tennessee Campaign unfolded in the spring of 1864. A transplant from the Army of Northern Virginia, Hood joined the western Army of Tennessee after recovering from a wound at Chickamauga. Following the army's long withdrawal through north Georgia in the face of pressure from Sherman, the Confederate government called for a change in leadership, tapping Hood for an impossible job: saving Atlanta.

# About the Author

**William Lee White** is a park ranger at the Chickamauga and Chattanooga National Military Park, where he gives tours and other programs at the Chickamauga and Lookout Mountain battlefields. He is the author of *Bushwhacking on a Grand Scale: The Battle of Chickamauga September 18-20, 1863*, along with several articles and essays on topics related to the Western Theater, and he is the editor of *Great Things Are Expected of Us: The Letters of Colonel C. Irvine Walker, 10th South Carolina Infantry CSA*, and the lost fragment of Major General Patrick Cleburne's October 1864 diary published in *The Tennessee Campaign of 1864*. Over the years, he has spoken to and led tours for many roundtables, historical societies, and other history-minded groups.